Supervision for SUPER VISION

Prof. Dr. K. Chandrakandan
Dr. C. Karthikeyan
Er. C. Venkatesan
Er. C. Balaji Babu

AUTHORSPRESS

Worldwide Circulation through Authorspress Global Network
First Published 2002
by Authorspress

E-35/103, Jawahar Park
Laxmi Nagar, Delhi-110 092

e-mail: authorspress@yahoo.com
quantum_soul@mantramail.com

Typeset in NewCenturySchlbk by Chitra Computers

Supervision for SUPER VISION
ISBN 81-7273-097-7

Printed in India at Tarun Offset, Delhi.

Preface

This is a unique collection of theories and practices of supervision, as management without supervision is sterile and futile. This book focuses on the fundamentals, theories, and practices of supervision in the context of development administration and management. Supervision is an art of directing the efforts or harnessing the energy of human beings to attain organisational goals / objectives with high efficiency. Supervisors are found in every line of work organisation,.that is to say, social and economic service to community / business organisations. The nature of supervision varies with the kind of the work to be supervised, the type of people to be supervised, the extent of the supervisory responsibility and the level of supervision. The significance of supervision in developmental organisation is felt widely and it is the right time to think of a book on this line.

This book comprises seven chapters. The first chapter covers the fundamental aspects of supervision, viz., definition, development of the concept, relationship with administration, nature and approaches, principles, levels, styles, techniques and theories. Chapter two deals with the functions and attributes of supervisor in a developmental organisation. This chapter includes manager v/s supervisor, functions, principal responsibilities, principles, performance appraisal, result achievement, rating scales, personal characteristics and qualities of a good supervisor and the desired traits of good supervisor.

Chapter three is about the supervisor-subordinate relationship and supervision in development programmes. This chapter focuses about the motivation of subordinates, assistance to subordinates, relation with superiors, improving relationship, and objectives of supervisor. The next chapter is about the decision making in supervision. This emphasises the concept of decision, elements in decisionmaking, nature and characteristics of decision, decisionmaking process, steps in decision making, types of management decision styles, types of decisions, types of managerial decisions, characteristics of programmed and non-programmed decisions, decision-making conditions, rational decisionmaking, techniques in decision making, advantages and disadvantages of group decision making and ways to improve decision making.

The basic managerial functions have their life time firmly rooted in the organisational heartbeat of communication only. Chapter five is tailored towards this end. This covers the importance, purpose, and elements of organisational communication, flow of communication, limitation, forms of organisational communication network, communication skills, barriers, and breakdown in communication.

Coordination is the common thread running throughout the management functions. Chapter six is devoted on this aspect. This covers the definitions, approaches, basic functions, importance, principles, effectiveness in management, techniques, and constraints of coordination in development organisation.

The last chapter is on the role of supervision in extension administration. Research findings on this subject were incorporated.

Besides this, three annexures were provided about the following:

i) Organisational set-up of the Directorate of Agriculture.

ii) The art of delegation.

iii) Model question papers on this subject.

This book would be useful to organisational managers, administrators, students and researchers in the field of HRD, management, public administration, social sciences, agricultural extension, sociology and those preparing for All-India competitive examinations such as IAS, IPS, IFS, ARS, etc.

Authors

Contents

1

Supervision—Principles, Techniques and Theories

The word supervision is derived from Latin, meaning to oversee. The main essence of management is to get the work done by the people by directing them in the right perspective. In management, supervision means overseeing the sub-ordinates at work with authority and with an aim to guide the employee, if he is erring. It means subordinates should be led so as to be directed towards the common goal.

A formal organisation has, in general, three levels of direct participants. First there is the top level of leadership, which may be centred in one person or a group of persons such as a governing board. These are the policy makers, usually known as the top administrators. The second important group is the rank and file of members (the subordinate staff) who carry on the actual work of the organisation. The third major group is a body of functionaries who carry out the policies and directions of the leadership, and who supervise and control the activities of the rank and file. They are generally called supervisors, executives, etc.

DEFINITIONS OF SUPERVISION

Supervision refers to the direct and immediate guidance and control of subordinate in the performance of their task.

(*Viteless*, 1976)

According to Halsey (1946), supervision is selecting the right person for each job; arousing in each person an interest in his work and teaching him how to do it; measuring and rating performance to be sure that teaching has been fully effective; administering correction where this is found to be necessary and transferring to more suitable work or dismissing those for whom this proves ineffective; commending whatever praise is merited or rewarding for good work; and finally fitting each person harmoniously into the working group, all done fairly, patiently and tactfully so that each person is caused to do his work skilfully, accurately, intelligently, enthusiastically and completely.

According to Appley (1969), supervision is to close the gaps between desired performance and actual human performance.

Supervision is generally defined as the art of directing the activities of human beings. Supervision is leadership and the development of leadership within groups which are co-operative (Vashist, 1994).

According to Collings (1959), supervision is a process by which workers are helped to do their jobs with increasing satisfaction to themselves, to the people with whom they work, and to the agency.

Development of Supervision

Before 1900	: Administrative inspection. Teachers considered as instruments to be supervised by administration.
Turn of the century	: Supervision by specialists. New subjects required services of specialists. Supervision continued to be arm of administration.
The 1920's	: Scientific supervision. Supervision was to discover 'laws' of education and apply them through teachers. Research and measurement were

	the domain of supervisers. Teachers were to apply findings.
The 1940's	: Supervision as Democratic Human Relations Teachers had feelings and emotions which were appealed to for action. Emphasis was given to personal determination of ends.
After 1940's	: Supervision through reason, practical intelligence.
Reason	: The specification of desired outcomes and appropriate behaviour necessary to their attainment.
Practical intelligence	: Action through wide participation of all concerned in the processes of inquiry and the judgement of outcomes.
Current trends	: Supervision carried out by the "Workshop way of working".

Contrasts between Traditional and Modern Supervision

Traditional	*Modern*
1. Inspection	Study and analysis
2. Teacher focused	Aid material, method, teacher, pupil and environment focused
3. Visitation and Conference	Many diverse functions
4. Random and haphazard or a meagre, formal plan	Definitely organised and planned
5. Imposed and authoritarian	Derived and cooperative
6. One person usually	Many persons

Relation between Administration and Supervision

Burton and Bureckner point out that early literature devoted considerable space to the question: "can or should?". Supervision should be separated from administration. The two can be separated arbitrarily only for the sake of analysis. A separation in function is impossible. Many of the functions of the supervisor are administrative in nature and conversely the administrator must carry out supervisory functions.

The following facts derived from the studies of activity are of value in clarifying thinking:

1. All supervisory duties are performed at one time or another by administrative officers. Many administrative duties are performed from time to time by supervisory officers.
2. A number of duties are difficult to classify as one or the other despite restricted definitions of administration and supervision.
3. Great differences exist between administrators not alone in their sharing of supervisory duties but in their control of supervisory officers and duties.

Nature and Approaches of Supervision

The nature of supervision varies with the kind of the work to be supervised, the type of the people to be supervised, the extent of the supervisory responsibility and the level of supervision.

Conventional Approach

Until fairly recently the "autocratic supervisor was the order of the day". The popular oration of supervision was expressed in terms of "the power to command, the exercise of authority or ability to dominate". This approach may be termed as "task oriented, or content oriented or the conventional conception of management task".

The viewpoints of this approach may be:

1. Supervision is a process of directing people, motivating them, controlling their actions, modifying their behaviour to fit the needs of the organisation.
2. Without this active intervention by supervisors, people would be passive or even resistant to organisational needs. They must therefore be persuaded, rewarded, punished, controlled and their activities must be directed.
3. The average man is by nature indolent, he works as little as possible.
4. He lacks ambition, dislikes responsibility, prefers to be led.
5. He is inherently self-centred, indifferent to organisational needs.
6. He is by nature resistant to change.

Results of Autocratic Supervision Based on Conventional Approach

1. Most employees develop a sense of frustration, and finally they feel insecure in their job.
2. Work slows down or stops completely when the supervisor is away.
3. The employee's needs for a feeling of importance and satisfaction are not met.
4. Employees are to be kept dependent on the supervisor, thus they have no opportunity to show initiative.
5. Employees frequently either become aggressive or alternatively identify closely with supervisor.

New (Democratic) Approach

With the change of times, with the increase in the general educational level, and with the findings emerging from social sciences, the typical conventional pattern of dictation is yielding place to one of consultation based on the art and science of human relations, just as despotism in ruling mankind has been replaced by democracy, with the gradual enlightenment of humanity. Thus a new concept of supervision has developed which is "group-oriented" or employee-centred "rather than "production-centred". The viewpoint of this new approach is that, while the conventional theory places exclusive reliance upon external control of human behaviour, the new theory relies heavily on self-control and self-direction.

Results of Democratic Approach

1. Employees produce a larger quantity and higher quality of work.
2. Individual and group morale are high.
3. Employees have a highly developed sense of group feeling.
4. Employees' basic needs to participate and to feel important are met.
5. Employees feel secure.
6. Employees seldom become aggressive.
7. The supervisor finds that less supervision is necessary.

Principles of Supervision

According to F.E. Rogers and Olmsted:

1. Supervision is an essential part of administration, integral to it, but not identical with it.
2. Supervision is a cooperative activity. It takes place through the shared ideas, effects and experiences of all staff members, cooperation provides an opportunity for the growth of the supervisor as well as for the growth of the employee.
3. Supervision is ordinarily concerned with the cooperative improvement of the softing in which learning takes place.

It seeks improved methods of teaching and creates a physical, social, psychological, climatic condition favourable to learning.

4. Planning is fundamental to supervision. It is cooperative in nature and orderly in procedure from the inception of an idea to the extension of a series of activities.
5. Supervision is creative, not prescriptive. It determines procedures in the light of the needs of each situation. It provides an opportunity for originality and self-expression. It is scientific in its approach to problem solving.
6. Supervision substitutes leadership for authority. It is based on the democratic philosophy that respects individual differences and that assumes people are capable of growth.

   It stimulates initiative, self-reliance, and individual responsibility. Opportunities are provided for the cooperative formulation of policies, plan and goals.
7. There is an art to be learned for the successful practice of supervision. It is primarily the art of building creative human relationships.
8. Successful supervision is measured in terms of the qualitative growth of those being supervised.
9. Supervision provides for the establishment of extension objectives and goals and a means for comprehensive and systematic evaluation of the extension programme.

Principles Governing the Nature of Supervision

(Vashist S.R. 1994)

1. Supervision is ordinarily concerned with improving the setting for learning in particular.
2. Administration and supervision considered functionally cannot be separated or set off from each other . The two are

coordinate, correlative, complementing mutually shared functions in the operation of educational systems.

3. Good supervision is based on philosophy and science.
4. Supervision will be sensitive to ultimate aims and values, to policies with special reference to their adequacy.
5. Good supervision is based upon the democratic philosophy.
   a. Supervision will respect personality and individual differences between personalities, will seek to provide opportunities for the best expression of each unique personality.
   b. Supervision will provide full opportunity for the cooperative formulation of policies and plans, will welcome and utilise free expression and contributions from all.
   c. Supervision will stimulate initiative, self-reliance, and individual responsibility on the discharge of their duties.
   d. Supervision will substitute leadership for authority.
6. Good supervision will employ scientific methods and attitudes in so far as those methods and attitudes are applicable to the dynamic social processes of education.
7. Good supervision will be creative and not prescriptive.
   a. Supervision will determine procedures in the right of the needs of each supervisory teaching-learning situation.
   b. Supervision will provide an opportunity for the exercise of originality and for the development of unique contributions, of creative self-expression, and will seek latent talent.
   c. Supervision will deliberately shape and manipulate the environment .
8. Good supervision proceeds by means of an orderly, cooperatively planned and executed series of activities.

9. Good supervision will be judged by the result it secures.
10. Good supervision is becoming professional. It is increasingly seeking to evaluate its personnel, procedure and results; it is moving towards standards and towards self-supervision.

Principles Governing the Purposes of Supervision

1. The ultimate purpose of supervision is the promotion of pupil growth, and hence eventually the improvement of society.
2. A second general purpose of supervision is cooperatively to formulate and carry out an educational policy and plan designed to achieve the ultimate goal.
3. A third general purpose of supply leadership in securing continuity and constant readaptation in the educational programme over a period of years: from level to level within the system; and from one area of learning experience and content to another.
4. The immediate purpose of supervision is cooperatively to develop favourable settings for teaching and learning and for doing the things.
   a. Supervision, through all means available will seek improved methods of learning and doing the work.
   b. Supervision will coordinate and integrate all efforts and materials; will give continuity.
   c. Supervision will create a physical, social and psychological climate or environment favourable to learning and doing the work.
   d. Supervision will enlist the cooperation of all staff members in serving their own needs and those of the situation.
   e. Supervision will aid, inspire, lead and develop that security which liberates the creative spirit.

Levels of supervision principles and processes

Level	*Social theory*	*Programme of supervision*	*Methods of supervision*	*Staff relationship*
Free purposeful activity				
A.				
1. By individuals leaders, experts at work on frontier problems	Democracy leader devotees himself to a problem for common good.	Self-supervision eventual contribution to group programme.	Continuous self-initiated attention to needs new discoveries, etc.	General supervisor climate. It stimulates individual supervisors on consultancy basis
2. Any individual working, studying and striving to improve his own work	Democracy individual reconstructs his contribution to welfare of the group.	Self - supervision eventual contribution to group programme.	Continuous self-survey	General supervisor climate. It stimulates individual supervisors on consultancy basis

(Cont...)

B. Cooperatively within groups	Democracy; co-operative group formulation of policy and programme Participation in predeter-mined plan	Cooperatively derived from situation and based on needs	Continuous co-operatives self survey of needs aid on service-basis	Training guidance relationship dominant.
A. Liberal policy	Benovolent autocracy learning towards democracy, voluntary participation in carrying out plan of supervisors would be hoped for.	Predetermined. Plan is imposed but suggestions and modifications within it are given a hearing.	Participation of all is invited in carry-out plan from central office	Inspection and training guidance are prominent
B. Conservative Policy	Paternalism directed and controlled partricipation in plan of supervisors	Predetermined plan is imposed minimum only of suggestion and modification received.	With little or no consideration of individual needs.	Inspection and checking of performance. Imposition of practices

Styles of Supervision

According to the Michigan researches, there are two distinct styles of supervision:

1. Employee-centred supervision and
2. Production-centred supervision

Employee-centred supervision

A supervisor is said to be employee-centred if he considers supervision of his people, rather than expediting production to be his main job. His method of getting the work done by the people is to satisfy them by providing them the necessary information, material and organisation and guiding them on the work as to how the work is to be accomplished. He does not keep a close watch on how the work progresses. He believes the workers and assumes that the workers are responsible enough to assume their own responsibilities without any pressure of looking over, though he is always available for any technical assistance and for securing necessary facilities from the management.

Production-centred supervision

A supervisor is rated as production-centred if he considers the production his main job and regards his men primarily. The instruments for getting the work done rather than as human beings with needs and emotions similar to his own. He is more detached and more objective than the employee-centred supervisor. He does not hesitate to insert himself in the daily flow of work, if he thinks that work is not going in a way. He is hard to his instructions and does not like any deviation from them.

Employee-centred vs Production-centred Supervision

The problem as to whether the supervisor should be employee-centred or production-centred should be decided on the merit of the individual case. The Michigan studies have made it clear that the employee-centred supervision is more effective than the production-centred supervision. The studies show that the higher productivity of the expense of worker's dignity is the surest way of delecating the very purpose. They have also brought out the fact that interest and responsibility on the part of the workers are affected by the behaviour of the supervisor which follows the attitude of workers towards production and also affects the group motivation and morale; researches concluded that the employee-centred supervision definitely leads to higher productivity and greater employee satisfaction. This fact is not confirmed by the other researches. According to other researches production-centred supervision under certain conditions may yield as good a production record, at least in the short run but the Michigan team maintains that in the long run the employee-centred groups develops into a better equipped and a more healthy group and is better able to maintain its productivity gains than the production-centred group .

TECHNIQUES OF SUPERVISION

Techniques of supervision means the methods used to get the work done by the workers. These techniques are:

1. Autocratic technique
2. Democratic technique
3. Free-rein technique

Autocratic Techniques

Under this technique all the powers of supervision are concentrated in the hands of supervisors and "rule of thumb" is a weapon they use indiscriminately. A supervisor has full control over his subordinates. He behaves as a hard task master and imposes his will off and on. This technique is not used in modern times because the human concept of labour has its recognition in modern times and workers have full liberty to convey their feelings to the movement; they cannot work as a machine. The supervisor should also avoid the use of this technique as it tends to destroy the very idea of the organisation.

Democratic Technique

Under this technique, democratic principles are followed. Workers are taken into confidence. The superior, though in charge of the workmen and responsible for getting the work done, is not allowed to act according to his whims and temperament and liking and dislikings. Instead, consultation, counselling, group discussion are the roles of supervisors. The workers are encouraged to suggest the best ways and means of doing the job. If suggestion proves faithful, it is recognised by the organisation. It helps motivate the workers and heightens the morale. This technique is generally followed in modern industries.

Free-rein Technique

This technique is just the reverse to the autocratic technique. Under this technique the policies, programmes and objectives of the organisations are fully explained to the workers. It is also known to them what, when and who has to do the job. A time schedule is also given. Now the workers are free to work according to the instructions and methods already explained. The supervisor aims at guiding the workman, he does not interfere in his work. It is up to the worker to show the best results. It seems to be the best technique but success of this technique depends on unrestricted supervision and efficient and effective communication system which are generally not present.

So, no technique of supervision is said to be the best. Indeed, supervision is an individual trait and wisdom, and the supervisor should develop his own technique according to the circumstances. His technique may differ from situation to situation, from work to work, from individual to individual, from group to group, and from organisation to organisation.

THEORIES OF SUPERVISION

Supervisory use of motivational theories can be useful for broadening the supervisors' understanding so that he can practise them to get the job done. To fully appreciate the changes that have been placed in management philosophies it is important to examine a few additional theories. The first one will be Theory X and Theory Y of Douglas Mcgregor. He classified traditional theories of management (Theory X) and new development (Theory Y).

X Theory

1. The average human being has an inherent dislike of work and will avoid it if he can.
2. Due to this, most people must be coerced, controlled, directed and threatened with punishment to get them to put out a day's work for a day's pay.
3. The average human being prefers to be directed, because he doesn't like responsibility, has relatively little ambition, and wants security above all.

Y Theory

1. People enjoy work as naturally as they enjoy play.
2. Most people are capable of exercising self-control and self-direction if they are motivated to achieve a goal.
3. The average worker will not only accept but will actively seek responsibility.

Gellerman's Theory

Gellerman's speaks of two major styles of management: (1) the method involving coercion, threat of dismissal, and (2) the method involving compensation, reward. Both these methods are based on the assumption that people must be subjected to external controls to be productive.

Reinforcement Theory

The reinforcement theory is a behavioural point of view in which learning can be defined as changed behaviour resulting from or accompanying practice or experience. Learning is analysed in terms of observable events and not in terms of internal factors.

The supervisor applies these theories in staff learning so that:

1. Stimuli are presented to change the environment to ensure a change in behaviour.
2. Behaviour changes occur on the part of the learner.
3. The behaviour is predetermined, intended and explicit.

Lifecycle Theory of Supervisor

This theory presumes that individuals and the newly formed group of employees move through progressive stages of emotional maturity. A newly formed development will probably require tight, autocratic supervision. A fully mature group, one that really knows its strengths and weeknesses, can be trusted to respond most effectively to participative supervision.

Two-factor Theory (Herzberg)

Herzberg says that every human being has two motivational

tracks: (1) a lower-level one, animal in nature and bent only on surviving and (2) a higher level one, uniquely human and directed toward adjusting to oneself. Herberg labels the first set of motivations "hygiene" or maintenance factors. We need to satisfy them, the reasons to keep alive, people try to avoid pain and unpleasantness in life; they do the same on the job.

Expectancy Theory

It suggests that the supervisor's main job is to strengthen the arrows in the expentency theory diagram.

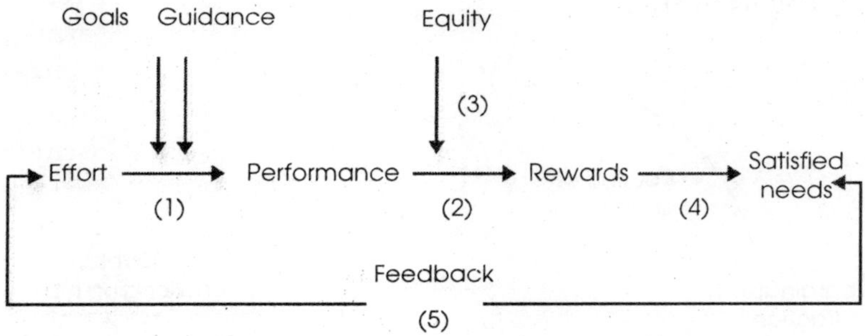

Specifically the supervisor (1) makes it easier for the subordinate to convert efforts into productivity. (2) Increases the likelihood that higher productivity will be rewarded. (3) Ensures that rewards are distributed more equitably. (4) Possibly even changes the values (in terms of satisfaction) of these rewards to employees. (5) Helps improved feedbacks.

Together these activities should increase the subordinates' work efficiency, the rewards they receive from effort and their general job satisfaction. In short, subordinates should expect higher effort to lead to valued rewards.

Contingency Theory

The heart of contingency theory consists of the following insights:

1. The key relationship between structure and both satisfaction and productivity may be curvilinear (contested hypothesis). If subordinates receive too little structure, that is, if they are provided too little information as to what they are supposed to do or how they are supposed to do it, they become anxious.

   Increase in their structure provides them more guidance and their satisfaction will also increase. But increase structure too much beyond point A on the chart above and helpful guidance turns into oversupervision; when this occurs, employees become frustrated and satisfaction begins to drop.

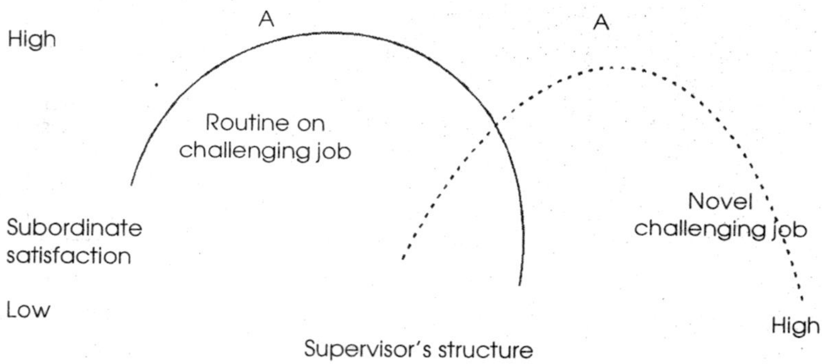

2. The ideal amount of structure (Point A) varies from one situation to another. Thus, workers on a routine job will wan't much less structure than those on new, complex tasks. The latter will have much more guidance from the boss.
3. The relationships between support and either production or satisfaction are more complex. By large, the more support the better, but in some instances, an increase in support will make a big an difference; in other instances extra support may have little impact (e.g., for a highly dependent worker).
4. Appropriate supervisory behaviour changes almost from minute to minute.

2

Functions and Attributes of a Supervisor

The term supervisor has its roots in Latin, where it means "looks over", in Germany the supervisor is still called a *vorarbeiter* which means "fore worker".

Anyone of the first level of management who has the responsibility for getting the "hands-on-the-work" employees to carry out the plans and policies of higher-level management is a supervisor.

The federal laws of the United States provide definitions of a supervisor: any individual having authority, in the interest of the employer, to hire, transfer, suspend, lay off, recall, promote, discharge, assign, reward, or discipline, other employees or responsibility to direct them or to adjust their grievances or to effectively recommended such action, if in connection with the foregoing the exercise of such authority is not of a merely routine or clerical nature, but requires the use of independent judgement (Taft Hartley Act, 1947).

SUPERVISOR AND MANAGER

Supervisor and Manager are two terms used interchangeably for describing different functions of the management process.

Managers	Supervisors
1. Managers can deal with many different variables, such as people, machines, money, events, time, markets and systems.	Supervisors deal primarly with people and their attendent problems within an operating organisation.
2. Managers create and maintain an internal environment in a company so that other people can perform efficiently in their efforts towards the achievement of the group's goal.	Supervisors, on the other hand, are managers whose major function emphasises leading, coordinating and directing the work of others in order to achieve the group's goals.

Functions of Supervisor

The supervisor performs many important functions in the work organisation.

1. He is the first line manager responsible for implementing the policies, plans and procedures established by management.
2. Defining the work roles of his subordinates.
3. His role in job relations.
4. Implementing policies and programmes.
5. His role as a leader.

The supervisors as a first line manager

The supervisor plays an important role in management. He is the official manager of his work group. He operates at the lowest level of management. He implements many of the objective plans, policies and procedures which are formulated for him by the levels of management above his. He inturn has the authority to determine objectives plans, procedures, rules and methods, provided that these are consistent and coordinated with those of his superiors.

Defining the Work Roles of His Subordinates

The basic nature of the work roles is fixed by the particular type of business which the organisation undertakes. The type of business determines to a greater extent, the type of personnel who are needed to perform the work rules. The supervisor can study the nature of the job, devise methods for undertaking the tasks. Lay, down specifications for the qualities and qualifications needed for effective performance of the work role. He can ensure the Effective performance of the work role by proper selection of persons with the correct skills as training, by appropriate induction and others, and where necessary by correction. Also the supervisor has an important role in reallocating persons who do not fit their work roles. He is responsible for initiating, transfers, demotions and dismissals.

He may also recommend the promotion of those who can perform more important work roles. His decisions should relate both to the organisational needs of the work roles to be performed and to the claims of his subordinates for fair consideration.

His role in job relations

The formal definition of the work role and its allocation to a particular individual does not assure that he will behave in the way expected of him. The management and the supervisor have certain expectations with respect to the effort performed in terms of quantity and quality of work, the cost of and the degree of safety with which operations are performed. An individual may not perform up to these expectations because of his attitude, interests and personality. One of the functions of the supervisor is to handle individuals in their varying attitudes, to secure their cooperation and to motivate them so far as it is humanly possible. The supervisor may need to resolve individual problems and to cancel his subordinate: so that they behave in a constructive way. The supervisor must have a good understanding of human nature.

It is not only his subordinates whom a supervisor must try to understand and with cooperation. He has relations with fellow supervisors, with other managers, and with his own superior. The handling of his own immediate superior is no easy task and many conflicts are likely to arise.

So a clear perception of his own work role and his authority is necessary to achieve his objectives.

Implementing policies and programmes

An important element in the modern supervisory role is one of implementing policies and programmes which relate to personnel. The supervisor must also implement programmes which are designed to develop or safeguard his subordinates. Safety programmes are designed to prevent subordinates injuring themselves.

Supervisor as a leader

The supervisor is not only a representative of management to his men, he is also a representative of the men to his management. One of the most important functions of the supervisor is that of a leader. He is responsible for setting objectives for the group, and for determining some of the principal methods of reaching the objectives. He has a responsibility as leader to see that the change is implemented without upsetting the group too greatly.

According to H. Nissen, there are three principle aspects of the supervisor's work and equipment, namely.

1. Technical, i.e., familiarity with the know-how of the work to be supervised.
2. Institutional, i.e., familiarity with the policies and procedure governing the work to be supervised.
3. Human, i.e., the ability to deal tactfully with the worker under supervision.

Nissen gives the following list of eleven principal duties of a supervisor:

1. To understand the duties and responsibilities of his own position.
2. To plan the execution of the work.
3. To divide the work among the subordinates and to direct and assist them in doing it.
4. To improve work methods and procedures.
5. To improve his own knowledge as a technical expert and leader.
6. To train the personnel.
7. To evaluate the performance of the employees.
8. To correct mistakes and solve employee problems and develop discipline in the employees.
9. To keep subordinates informed about policies and procedures of the organisation and about the changes to be made.
10. To cooperate with colleagues and to seek advice and assistance when needed.
11. To deal with employee suggestions and complaints.

Responsibilities and Principles of Extension Supervisors

Those who happen to work as supervisors in the extension programme can improve the working by adopting the following responsibilities and principles:

1. Make a job analysis and develop a job description for each position.
2. Help employees to develop a feeling of responsibility towards the job.
3. Make the job as meaningful as possible.

   This challenges each employee to develop and use his potential capacities.
4. Develop methods for making work easier without lowering the standards of the organisation.

5. Make vivid to the employee the important reason why a given standard needs to be met.
6. Provide a sense of security and an opportunity for mutual understanding.
7. Recognise and act on the fact that employees need to have some part in establishing good human relations in the organisation.
8. Provide the employee participation in decision making.
9. Be employee-centred.
10. Use the consultative approach.
11. Avoid favouritism.
12. Give clear, precise, timely and acceptable orders.
13. Give orders that correspond to the employer's development and that match the level of his sense of responsibility.
14. Have frequent contacts with employees.
15. Think of functions and not only of functionaries.
16. Think of both function and personnel in relation to the objectives of the organisation.
17. Take the long view and not just meet each situation as though it existed only for the present.

Supervisory Performance Judged by Higher Management

It will be judged by two general measures:

a) How will you manage the various resources made available to you to accomplish your assignments?
b) How good are the results that you get from them?

Management of resources

There are the things that in effect set you up in business as a supervisor:

1. Facilities and equipment, such as a certain amount of floor space, desks, benches, tools, production machinery, computer terminals, and microfiche readers.
2. Energy power and utilities, such as heat, light air-conditioning, electricity, steam, water and compressed air, conservation as the principal measures of effectiveness here.
3. Materials and supplies such as raw materials, parts and assemblies used to make a product and operating. Supplies such as lubricants, stationery. Getting the most from every scrap of material and holding waste to the minimum are prime makers here.
4. Human resources such as workforce in general and your employees in particular. Since you do little or nothing with your hands, your biggest job is to see that these people are productively engaged at all times.
5. Information such as that made available by staff developments or found in operating manuals, specifications sheets, and blueprints. Your success often depends on how well you can a utilise the data and know-how made available to you through these sources.
6. Money; at all above can be measured by how much they cost, although the actual cash will rarely pass through your hands.

   Nevertheless, supervisors are expected to be prudent in decisions that affect expenditures and may have to justify these in terms of savings or other benefits.

ATTAINMENT OF RESULTS

It follows that if you manage each of your resources well, you should get the desired results. Whatever your particular area of responsibility and whatever your organisation, you can be sure that you will be judged in the long run by how well you meet these three objectives.

Output of Production

Specifically, your department will be expected to turn out a certain amount of work per day, per week and per month. It will be expected that this will be done on time, that you will meet delivery schedules and project deadline;

Quality and Workmanship

Output volume alone is not enough. You will also be judged by the quality of the work your employees perform, whether it be measured in terms of the number of product defects, service errors or customer complaints.

Costs and Budget Control

Your output and quality efforts will always be restricted by the amount of money you can spend to carry them out.

Universally supervisors attest to the difficulty in living up to cost and budget restraints.

A Supervisor's Rating Scale

A supervisor may rate himself as regards his ability to supervise his subordinates, on these points:

1. Forcefulness (giving order properly, keep in touch)
2. Ability to inspire confidence, respect, impartial, self-control
3. Ability to take a personal interest in the men
4. Ability to get the work done correctly
5. Ability to get and use the ideas
6. Ability to be one of the men
7. Ability to lead rather than boss over the men
8. Ability to develop team work

9. Ability to show kindliness without being considered easy
10. Ability to reprimand properly
11. Ability to keep from worrying
12. Ability to delegate work properly
13. Ability to call forth the best efforts of the men
14. Ability to train men on the job
15. Ability to make a new men feel at home
16. Self-confidence
17. Accident prevention.

ATTRIBUTES OF A SUPERVISOR

Personnel Characteristics

Competence to perform his job technically

The first line supervisor must have a working knowledge of the job being performed by the men he supervises.

Initiative and drive

A characteristic of a well-managed organisation is that each member will carry forward the execution of his responsibilities expeditiously within his delegated authority. This implies that each manager or supervisor should possess the characteristics of initiative and drive.

Enjoyment of responsibility

A leader must enjoy carrying responsibility. This is another characteristic that is partly inherited and partly acquired. However it is sometimes the dividing line between the man who will make a successful supervisor and the one who will not.

Decision making ability

Decision making ability is related to the preceding characteristic. If a man enjoys carrying responsibility, it is likely that he will be a better decision maker than the one who shuns such a responsibility.

A good decision maker must be able to identify the problem, request the data required for a solution, make his decision and be willing to live with the result.

Emotional stability

A supervisor must have as much interest in the problems of others as he has in his own. Human beings tend to have problems and to interrelate with one another in such a manner as to cause additional problems. The supervisor is always the focal point of such conflicts. If he is going to lead these people toward a definable objective, he must be able to handle these conflicts without their affecting him emotionally.

Motivation

Motivation is somewhat similar to initiative and drive. A good supervisor is one who is susceptible to the motivation factors, and not overly affected by the dissatisfaction factors.

Vitality and endurance

The supervisors must have vitality and endurance. Due to the decision making involved, the supervisor is under considerably more stress than the followers, and he must respond to this stress with quietness and calmness.

Persuasiveness

The supervisor must be persuasive because he must communicate the plans and goals of the group. He must communicate any changes in these plans and goals. He must communicate to the group the orders that must be followed in the achievement of goals. Also, he must be sensitive to their needs and must satisfy these needs in such a manner that they will not interfere with the achievements of the goals.

Intellectual capacity

The supervisor must have an intellectual capacity that will

allow him to do many things. He must be creative in order to find ways to organise and inspire the group toward greater achievement. One of the main factors coupled with the intellectual capacity is common sense and judgement, without these the supervisor's intellectual capacity becomes quite ineffective.

Integrity and courage

Finally, perhaps two of the most important characteristics of all are integrity and courage. It is the common purpose of these goals that will ultimately unite the followers in their pursuit of the leader.

For successful supervisory behavioural patterns the supervisor should have personal behavioural patterns that can assist him to cope with his environment on the job. These behavioural patterns include his relationships:

1) With his group members
2) With higher management
3) With other departments
4) With unions
5) With technology and planning
6) With performance standards

Qualities of a Good Supervisor

J.M. Pfiffner has listed eight qualities which a good supervisor should have:

1. Command of job content: It means expert knowledge of the work to be supervised. The usefulness of this to a supervisor is obvious, but technical expertness by itself does not make a good supervisor.
2. Personal qualifications are a cooperative spirit, evenness of temper, and honesty. These qualities are more important in a supervisor than in almost others.
3. Teaching ability

4. General outlook of the supervisor should be one of faith in and enthusiasm for the work with which he is concerned so that he may be able to inspire and lead those under him.
5. Ethical and moral considerations require the supervisor to be free from the major vices generally condemned by society
6. Courage and fortitude imply that the supervisor should not be afraid of taking responsibility and acting decisively. This, however, must not degenerate into want or caution or foolhardiness.
7. Administrative technology means capacity to organise, co-ordinate and direct.
8. Curiosity and intellectual ability mean an attitude of mental alertness and flexibility and not being impervious to new ideas and practices.

Characteristics or Traits Desirable for Good Supervisors

Rogers, F. E. and Olmsted

1. Thoroughness
2. Fairness
3. Initiative
4. Tact
5. Enthusiasm
6. Emotional control
7. Intelligence
8. Integrity
9. Loyalty
10. Knowledge of the work
11. Flexibility and adaptability
12. Vision
13. Good judgement
14. Age

15. Physical vitality
16. Broad knowledge and interest
17. Resourcefulness
18. Cooperativeness
19. Common sense
20. Background
21. Ability to teach
22. Humanness
23. Language facility

REFERENCES

Bittel Lester R., 1985, *What every Supervisor should know*, Tata McGraw-Hill Publishing Company Ltd, New Delhi.

Dahama, O. P. and O. P. Bhetnegar, 1985, *Education and communication for development*, Oxford and IBH Publishing Co. Pvt Ltd, New Delhi.

Eckles, Robert W. Ronald L. Cermichael and Bernerd R. Scrchet, 1970, *Essentials of management for first line supervision*, John Wiley and Sons, Inc., New York.

Huneryager, S.G. and I.L. Heekmenn, 1967, *Human relations in management*, D.B. Taraporevala Sons & Co, Pvt Ltd, Bombay.

Lucio William H. and John D. Mencil 1969, *Supervision, A Synthesis of Thought and Action*, McGraw-Hill Book Company, New York.

Mamoria, C.B., 1980, *Personnel Management*, Himalaya Publishing House, Bombay.

Nubin Robert, 1979, *Human Relations in Administration,* Prentice Hall of India Pvt Ltd, New Delhi.

Reddy Adivi, 1993, *Extension education,* Sree Lakshmi Press Bapatla.

Rogers, F.E. and Olmsted Adn G., *Administration and Supervision, Extension Education.*

Roy Charles M. and Charles L Bison, 1983, *Supervision*, The Dryden Press, London.

Sharma, M.P., 1974, *Public Administration in Theory and Practice,* Kitab Mahal, Allahabad.

Vashist, S.R., 1994, *Principles of Educational Supervision,* Anmol Publications Pvt Ltd, New Delhi.

Yuill Bruce, 1967, *Supervision, Principles and Techniques,* George Allen and Unwin Ltd, United Kingdom.

3

Superior-Subordinate Relationship and Supervision in Development Programmes

The supervisor himself is a major influence on the behaviour of his own subordinates. The personality of the supervisor, the way he interprets policies of the organisation, and how effectively he performs his functions—all these factors have a great deal of bearing on the reaction of his subordinates. The supervisor has to understand the basic relations of work satisfaction, achievements, status and security of subordinates.

Research into supervisory work conducted shows that a supervisor needs to consider his subordinates, to help them at critical times, to sustain motivation by increasing job satisfaction, to avoid harsh corrective, evaluative and disciplinary decisions and to maintain their status and security. He needs to be capable of handling the problems of his subordinates.

The supervisor's performance is evaluated by his superior. In many situations the superior may differ in background, education and qualifications from those of the supervisor. However, it is not these factors which lead the supervisor into the greatest areas of conflict. It is the pressures on the supervisor which are generated by the specialist sections which cause him the greatest amount of anxiety and frustration. These sections sets goals, methods and standards for him and also tell him what he cannot do in order to achieve him.

There are other situations where a subordinate needs information to carry out his task and, he looks to the supervisor for his valuable and skilled ideas.

Studies show that supervisors who have high performance are ones who are mainly interested in their subordinates rather than the material or technical aspects of production or operations. They spend their time with their juniors discussing and communicating with them rather than trying to pressure them to greater efforts. The supervisors with low performance records try to instruct and order their subordinates more than do high performers.

Other studies suggest that it is best for the supervisor to create conditions which lead the subordinate to request information, instructions and orders from the superior, to approach himself critically about his performance and when he makes errors. The supervisor should view this as constructive behaviour on the part of his employees. Encouragement or even reward for honesty assists the subordinate in adjusting to the situation.

The supervisor needs to consider his subordinates' needs, which help in increased performance and satisfaction, and help in achieving the goals.

MOTIVATION OF SUBORDINATES

The supervisor makes use of incentives and security provided by the policies of organisation. He also sustains motivation by keeping the status of his subordinates as high as possible. He has both a negative and a positive role to perform; he must not use his authority to upset his subordinates; he can also follow a certain line of conduct to produce harmonious relations amongst his subordinates.

The supervisor should try to develop internal forms of motivation, a sense of achievement, a sense of completion, responsibility, recognition and self-development. He can do this by defining proper tasks, allowing subordinates freedom and discretion to decide methods, alleging them to complete tasks where possible, giving them praise for a job welldone and encouragement in the development of their skill, knowledge and work.

The supervisor needs to support the self-esteem of his subordinates. He has to recognise that his subordinates are different from each other and approach them according to their peculiarities, needs and wants. At the same time he needs to build up their identification with the work group. He accomplishes this by talking about things which are common to all. He has to maintain regular contact with his subordinates.

He has to be able to deal with his subordinates, who have problems, which may relate either to work or personal matters. He has to have emotional maturity to handle face-to-face problems. For this he needs empathetic qualities to understand the personal problem.

The supervisor is supposed to give his best possible cooperation and also receive it from others. He frequently stands alone in facing conflicts and problems; he is isolated not only from his subordinates but also from his fellow supervisors, his superior and staff department as well. Yet he has to lead and be oriented towards his subordinates, and he has to be well adjusted with the others in organisations.

Assistance to Subordinates

One of the basic functions of the supervisor is to facilitate the work of subordinates. Depending on the nature of the work in the organisation the supervisor does this by setting their objectives, schedule of work, organising the resource necessary to undertake the tasks, coordinating the arrival of materials, supplies and personnel, and maintaining adequate communication with all concerned.

It follows that a supervisor who fails to communicate about the objectives and plans, who does not schedule work effectively, or who fails to control is bound to lose the confidence of his subordinates. The subordinates become irritated and frustrated. There is noting worse for a subordinate anxious to get on with his task, than to find that materials are unavailable or the wrong equipment is on hand; the subordinates become confused when their supervisor cannot make up his mind about the work to be done.

There are times when subordinates need assistance to get out of a jam. A supervisor who can step in and assist the work gains the respect and thanks of his subordinates, and the confidence to trust him. He needs the intellectual qualities to work out ways of changing his subordinates' behaviour when this is necessary. He may need to be a persuader, a counsellor or at times, a politician to deal with certain problems that cannot be resolved in a more direct way.

Relations with Superior

The supervisor derives his authority from his superior who also holds him responsible for his tasks. He is therefore a subordinate and can be expected to behave as such a role demands.

The supervisor has his own personal needs and wants. He may seek greater recognition from management or want greater social status, and he wants pleasant working conditions. In order to reach the goals which arise out of these needs he is dependent to a large extent on his superior.

If his superior fails to see the problems of the supervisor and is oriented upwards, the supervisor also feels the same attitude towards his subordinates. The supervisor has another important instrument of power over his superior. In many situations the supervisor knows more about the work of the section than his superior. He is responsible for giving his superior advice in solving problems, feedback and making suggestions about future plans and procedures.

Finally, the supervisor has power over his superior by effectively carrying out the work of his section. In this connection, he acts as a leader, attending to his subordinates' wants and resolving the problems. Thus, he is greatly influenced by the behaviour of his superior in his effectiveness.

LINE AUTHORITY

The staff role is thus a role of service of managers. The staff is characterised by two important features, viz., it provides service to the line; it is record of right to command. Line authority is the heart of the relationship between superior and subordinates because it has the ultimate authority to command, act, decide, approve or disapprove all the organisational activities. Line authority is responsible for achieving the objectives of the organisation and naturally has the right and power to issue commands, to exact accountability and discipline for violation. It is characterised by two important features: the right to decide and the right to direct.

Improving the Supervisor-Subordinate Relationship

The following are some quidelines which may help in improving the relationship between the supervisor and the subordinates.

Clarity in relationship

In order to have clarity in the supervisor-subordinate relationship it is necessary to identify the duties and responsibilities of the particular staff function and personnel.

Acceptance of the subordinate advice

A supervisor should make adequate and proper use of subordinates. Full utilisation of staff service is necessary to maximise organisational effectiveness. Before taking action, the supervisor should mandatorily consult subordinates so as to derive the benefit of the counsel of the staffmen at an appropriate time. The subordinates, in turnes, should respond as soon as possible to request for help from line executives. They should keep themselves informed about the problems confronting the line, think ahead, make constructive plans and help the supervisor solve the difficult operating problems. The staff should make sure that the manager gets the credit for the results of their work.

An informed subordinate

Effective functioning of the organisation demands an informed staff, who can combine academic excellence with practical experience in a fruitful way. The informed staff must be treated as a vital working partner in the business. Requisite information must be provided, necessary resources must be supplied, participation in discussions and meetings in which staff has a legitimate concern, must be ensured, and finally, it should be informed of all decisions affecting its work.

Completed staff work

The principle of completed staff work, as suggested by L. Powell, demands that the staff expert must study and analyse a problem thoroughly so that the manager has only to accept or reject the proposal. Completed staff work implies three things: a careful study of the problem, listing of possible alternatives and clear recommendations based on facts compiled.

Supervision in Development Programmes

The supervisor performs many important function in the development programmes. He is responsible for implementing policies, programmes and procedures. He defines the work roles to his subordinates. He is the formal leader of his work group and in this capacity is responsible for improving human relations and morale.

The supervisor sees that his subordinates work together in order to achieve the programmes and targets. He has to motivate his subordinates, satisfy their work needs and build coordination. He has to try to resolve conflict. He has the authority to determine objectives, programmes, plans, procedures, methods, evaluation and monitoring of the development programmes. He has to perform the following functions:

Objectives

The supervisors frequently makes decisions. He has to define the goals of his subordinates' tasks, so that they contribute to the common objectives of the organisation.

Planning

The supervisors has to plan his work and the work of his subordinates. He may be required to schedule operations of programme to see that targets are met. Decisions have to be made within organisational policies. Procedures have to be observed and followed by both himself and his subordinates. Methods may be improved in order to conduct the programmes effectively and at a lower cost.

Organising

Within the limits of the budgets and schedules established for him, the supervisor is required to order and assemble the materials, supplies, equipment and personnel required to realise the length of programme. To do this he needs to know the activities and operations of the programmes.

Staffing

The supervisor has to define the work roles of his subordinates and allocate the work roles to the personnel based on their capacity and efficiency.

Directing

In accordance with the standards laid down in the programme, the supervisor directs his subordinates so that they may accomplish their respective targets within a specified time. He is unlikely to achieve this objective unless he exercises a great deal of leadership and motivation, and build teams put in subordinates. He has to use proper communication channels to maintain continual contact with his subordinates.

Controlling

Controlling involves the supervisor in fulfilling the targets — programme previously determined, checking and evaluating the performance of the subordinates as well as the programme, if necessary correcting the action from time to time by appropriate guidance. He makes out reports, keeps statistics and gives feedback to his superior. He analyses features and constraints of implement programmes.

Coordinating

To achieve coordination, the supervisor must understand the efforts involved in achieving the programme by his subordinates and he can appreciate the overall effort. For effective implementation the supervisor has to cooperate with the subordinates and give due credit for other person responsible for successive implementation programme.

Thus, the supervisor has to perform all the management functions for effective coordination.

4

Decision Making in Supervision

The managerial functions of planning, organising, controlling and coordinating are important concepts for the supervisory level of management to use and to understand. As important as these functions may be decisions may be decision making.

Decision making can be considered the process of choosing a course of action or activity designed to solve a specific problem or set of problems.

Decision making can be defined as an act of choice by the manager from among two or more possible alternative courses in a given situation.

There are two important factors in the process of decision making, viz., the underlying purpose and the circumstances in which the decision is made. The objective of a decision lies, in helping to reach the optimum and most desired result.

WHAT IS DECISION?

A decision is the selection of the course of action. It is a choice from among a set of alternatives. The word 'decision' is derived from the Latin words "de cise" which means "a cutting away or a cutting off" or in a practical sense to come to a conclusion. A decision may be the result of a hunch or a product of careful planning.

According to Felix M. Lopez (1977), "a decision represents a judgement, a final resolution of a conflict of needs, means or goals and a commitment to action made in the face of uncertainly, complexity and even irrationality."

Important Elements in Decision Making

The fundamental elements in decision making are intuition, facts (data), experience and authority. All these varying degrees, depending upon the nature of the problems and that of the decision making, find places as basis for decision making.

Intuition

This is generally the offspring of the innerfeelings of the decision maker because it is without any conscious attention or reasoning and concentration, etc., on the issues involved in the problem. The elements of intuition as a basis of decision making is useful in view of time expediency and making purposeful use of the decision making ability.

Facts (Data)

It is factual data having relevancy to a given situation that has been recognised as the most methodical, efficient and effective basis for reaching decisions.

Experience

Past experience of the decision maker, indicative of decisions made in a particular situation, varied types of people involved and general areas affected by decision weighs considerably with their decision maker and helps him in reaching accurate decisions.

Authority

There is existence of corelationship between authority and decision making. A decision involving authority is essentially in accordance with the company's policies and with general instructions as followed by the decision maker.

The advantages of decision making with the element of authority include ready accessibility and authenticity.

NATURE AND CHARACTERISTICS OF DECISIONS

Decisions are a composite of the following characteristics:

1. Process concept
2. Time sequence
3. Action commitment
4. Evaluation
5. Rationality

Process concept

The pattern of events and circumstances that has shaped a problem and the course it is likely take in future are factors of great influence in decision making. This process character of decision making is further elucidated by the time element in decision.

Time sequence

The facts and information pertaining to the past in which problems grew are gathered and the executive finds the need for a decision. As regards the present, the executive finds a number of alternative courses and chooses the one he considers the best. The time sequence is complete with the implementation of the decision and evaluation of results in the future.

Action commitment

Decisions often affect every part of the organisation and they must be acceptable to the people who are implement them. Decisions to be effective must be to the point, sound, accurate and appropriate. Such decisions in due course gain status of proceedings. We call this action commitment on the part of the supervisor making decisions.

Evaluation

a) The supervisor, giving due consideration of the pros and cons of two or more alternative course, chooses the one he considers best.

b) He weighs and measures the results of implementation of the decisions taken earlier.

Thus, evaluation becomes a continuous process in decision making.

Rationality

The supervisor, in the process of decision making has to use imagination, do a factual analysis of the past events and circumstances that led to a situation and take a realistic view of the whole thing. It is this approach that imparts rationality to his subordinates.

Decision making Process

According to Prof. Herbert Simon, there are phases:

a) *Intelligence activity*: In this phase an attempt is made to recognise and understand the nature of the problem, as well as search for the possible causes.

b) *Design activity*: Develop the alternate course of action and analyse in the light of known constraints.

c) *Choice activity*: The actual choice is made from out of the available alternatives at this stage.

Philip Marvin, G.P. Huber and F.A Shull have listed the following important phases in decision making process:

Explorative: The decision maker makes a realistic appraisal of current problems, challenges and what should be done to represent searching.

Speculative: The decision maker should analyse various factors affecting a decision, to which an appropriate response can be obtained.

Evaluative: He is expected to make cost-benefit analysis with various alternatives.

Selective: Making a choice among alternatives that would maximise the decision maker's total expected relative value.

In other words, decision making is the process by which the decision maker tries to jump over the obstacles placed between his current position and the desired future position.

STEPS IN DECISION MAKING PROCESS

The eight steps involved in decision process are:

Recognition and Analysis of the Problem

The first prerequisite of problem solving is to correctly define the problem, and what caused the trouble. The individual can recognise the (problem) trouble, but most often we see the symptoms rather than causal factors. After problem identification, the problem has to be analysed to know the relevant facts. These facts can be tangible factors like assignment of task, the work schedule, a conversation or an order given by the supervisor. Intangible factors includes morale, motivation, personal feeling, concepts and impressions.

Determination of Workable Solutions

Decision makers identify the specific problem to be solved and can isolate the facts pertinent to the problem; the next step must be to search for and state workable alternative solutions. State the all possible solutions and then eliminate the ones that are non-workable and select the one or two best workable solutions among the alternatives.

Identifying Key Uncertainties

Key uncertainties refer to the unknown that are the result of pure chance. Regardless of the solution chosen, the chance variable or key uncertainties would play an important role. This is helpful in making the final determination of decision making process.

Gathering Data

This includes identification, statement and analysis of the problem; a listing of all the alternative workable solutions and identification of key uncertainties of the problem. Now the decision maker knows where he is going, and how to get into the actual investigation of the problem.

Estimating the Value of Each Alternative

After gathering the data, the supervisor must analyse each alternative. He has to mentally test each alternative by judging the good and bad events that could occur if each alternative were put into effect.

Certain probability factors must be considered in the evaluation of each alternative. The question of the state of risk, the state of uncertainty, the state of ignorance have to be considered.

Choice of Solution

As the moment of truth arrives, the supervisor has to make a choice. He must make a choice among the alternatives or combination of the various alternatives. The choice can be assisted by the supervisor's experience, past judgement, advice from others or even a hunch but the fact remains, he must live with the outcome. Self-confidence is the best element for the supervisor to possess at this stage. He must be confident that he has the right problem, the most important workable solutions, the key uncertainties, proper data and proper evaluation of each alternative.

Action

The supervisor has to plan, organise and control the action so that the entire effort exerted on the proceeding steps is not wasted by poor practice of the managerial functions. The manager/supervisor has to work with and through others and this task may require communication motivation and leadership skills.

Follow-up

After the action is taken to implement the decision a follow-up and appraisal of the solution is necessary. This last step can take many forms, depending on the type of decision, the environment, working condition, desires of superiors, the workers involved and technical production problems.

Often reports are necessary for a supervisor's superior to learn of the decisions and outcome. Usually a follow-up will require a supervisory visit to the work station, desk or section of the change or activity initiated by the decision. The main

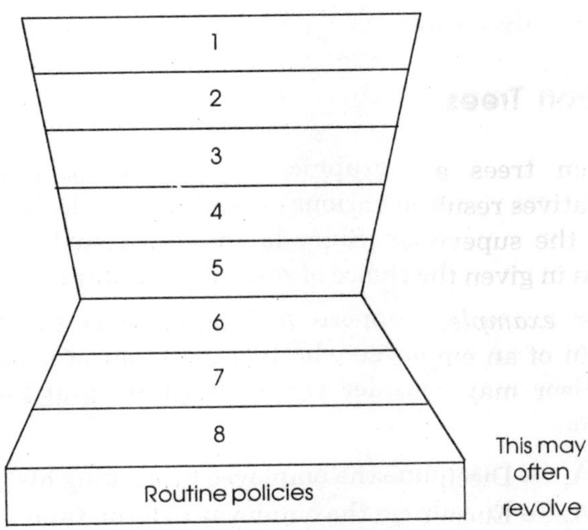

Steps in decision process

function of the follow-up is to determine that the problem has been resolved. If not, the supervisor may have to repeat the entire decision process, if a new problem has been generated by the solution. It is better to discover this failure during the follow-up period, rather than be unaware of a new problem provoked by the solution implemented.

STEPS IN DECISION MAKING

According to Jack Halloran and G.L. Funzi (1988) the decision making steps by acronym "ACTION" indicates six fundamental ones:

A = Analyse the problem and gather data.
C = Consider the alternative solutions.
T = Take action—select a solution.
I = Implement the solution.
O = Ongoing evaluation—conduct evaluation of the solution, encourage the feedback from employee.
N = Need for change. After you have tried the solution consider the need for modification of the original decision.

Decision Trees

Decision trees are graphic illustrations of how different alternatives result in various possibilities. A decision tree is an aid to the supervisor. Since it helps to visualise what could happen in given the choice of several possibilities.

For example: Suppose a supervisor is faced with the problem of an employee who has the habit of being late. The supervisor may consider three alternatives of handling the problem:

A_1 = Discipline the employee by docking his or her pay.
A_2 = Encourage the employee to be on time.
A_3 = Try the combination of both.

Types of Management Decision Styles

Victor Vroom and Philip Ylelton (1973) have developed a method to help managers decide when and to what extent they should involve subordinates in solving a particular problem. They isolated five types of decision making that represent a continuum from authoritarian decision making approaches (AI, AII) to consultative (CI, CII) to a fully participative one (G.II).

AI : Managers solve the problem or make the decision themselves, using information available at that time.

AII: Managers obtain the necessary information from subordinates, then decide on the solution to the problem themselves. They may or may not tell the subordinate what the problem is when they request information. The role played by subordinates in taking a decision is clearly one of providing the necessary information to managers rather than generating or evaluating alternative solutions.

CI: Managers share the problem with relevant subordinates individually getting their ideas and suggestions without giving them together as a group. Then the manager make the decision that may or may not reflect subordinate influence.

CII: Managers share the problem with subordinates as a group collectively, obtaining their ideas and suggestions. Then they make the decision that may or may not reflect subordinate influence.

GII: Managers share the problem with subordinates as a group. The manager and subordinates together evaluate alternatives and attempt to reach an agreement (consensus) on a solution. Managers do not try to influence the group to adopt their preferred solution and they accept and implement any solution that has the support of the entire group.

According to Mintz Berg (1973), focusing on strategy formulation, three styles or modes are identified.

Entrepreneurial style

Emphasis on growth, centralisation of power and dramatic innovation

Adoptive style

Involves gradual growth and often ad hoc adjustment to the changing environment.

Planning style

Emphasis is on rationality, rigorous analysis, anticipation of future, and strong involvement of staff analysis.

Decision styles

According to Hersey and Blanchard (1992), problem-solving and decision making styles not only describes four problem solving situations but also suggests four basic decision making styles, viz., (i) authoritative (ii) consultative (iii) facilitative and (iv) delegative. Each decision making style has a high probability of getting results depending on the readiness of the followers and the situations.

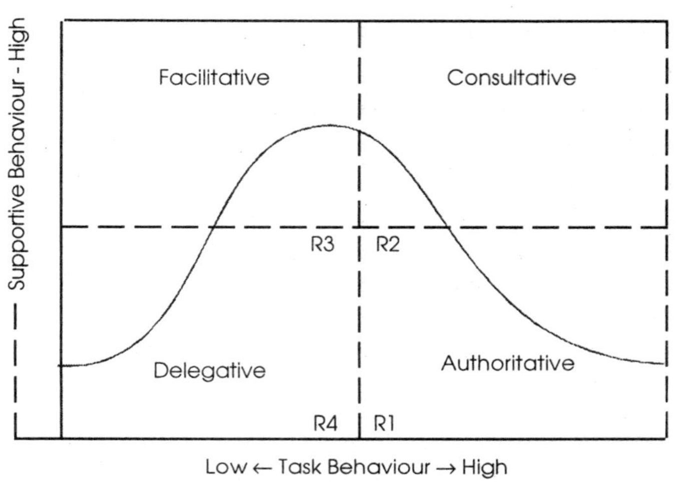

Problem-solving and decision making style

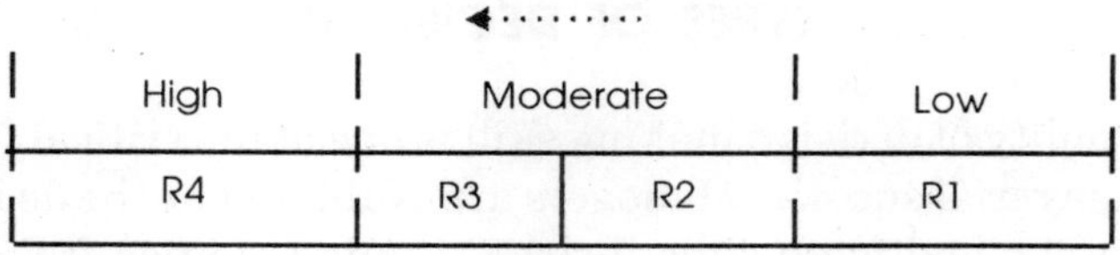

Problem-solving or decision making readiness

Authoritative Style

The leader or supervisor makes the decision and provides specific instructions to his followers or subordinates. The authoritative style requires a directive leader behaviour. Followers are usually not actively involved in determining the course of action. Therefore, they hear little about the decision until the manager announces it.

Consultative Style

The leader makes and explains the decision and provides an opportunity to have a dialogue and clarification with followers.

Facilitative Style

The leader shares the problem and mutually makes the decision with his followers. It is a cooperative effort in which the manager and the subordinates work together to reach a shared decision.

Delegative Style

The leader turns responsibility for his decision over to his followers. The followers who have the experience and information need to make the proper decision or recommendation.

TYPES OF DECISIONS

The quality of decision making skill is one of the critical factors in managerial success. Managers are evaluated by the decisions they make and more often, by the results obtained from their decisions. So it would be useful to distinguish between a decision made by managers at different levels in the organisation.

Rao and Narayanan (1996) have the following types of decisions:

Basic or Routine Decisions

Basic decisions are decisions concerning a unique problem or situation. They are one-time decisions demanding large investments. For example, decision about launching a new production plant or buying more advanced computer system are non-routine decisions. They require creativeness, intuition and good judgement on the part of managers. They are strategic decisions which affect the future of the organisation. As a manager progresses to higher levels the number of basic decisions increases.

On the other hand, routine decisions are repetitive in nature. They require little deliberation and are generally concerned with short-term commitments. They tend to have only minor effects on the welfare of the organisation. Generally, lower level managers look after such mechanical or operating decisions. For example, a supervisor can decide whether an employee's absence is excused or unexcused on the basis of personnel policy guidelines.

Personal or Organisational Decisions

According to Bernard, decisions can be divided on the basis of the environment in which they are made. The decision to study, watch T.V or retire early are examples. Such decisions pertain to managers or individuals, which affect the organisation in an indirect way.

Organisational decisions are made by managers in their official or formal capacity as controllers and allocators of organisational resources. These decisions are aimed at furthering the interests of the organisation. Results are measured in terms of the firm's earning, welfare of the employees and the economic health of the community.

Programmed and Unprogrammed Decisions

A programmed decision is one that is routine and repetitive. Rules and policies are established as a procedure for admitting items quickly. These decisions are relatively easy and simple for managers to make. However, routine procedures leave little room for manager to choose. Programmed decisions are usually made by lower lever personnel in organisations.

Non-programmed decisions deal with unique/unusual problems. The common features in these decisions are that they are novel and non-recurring and there is no readymade course of action to resort to. Since non-programmed decisions often involve broad, long-range consequences for the organisation, they are made by higher-level personnel only.

TYPES OF MANAGERIAL DECISIONS

An organisational set-up needs various types of decisions for its successful functioning. For convenience sake and easy understanding they may be classified as under.

According to Aggarwal (1984), the various types of decisions are:

Environmental Decisions

This type of decision has its primary objective as an integration of internal, intermediate and external environment into a cohesive whole, that is, total environment. The achievement of an objective enables an organisation to serve its membership better, must economically and effectively. These decisions have a great impact on decisions regarding the organisation's manifold objectives.

Objective Design Decisions

The general service level managers concentrate on the designing and formulation of their overall decisions for their organisation, and take action to see that in implementation of these decisions, as applied at all levels, other levels act accordingly.

Output Evaluation Decision

An organisation's environmental network matters considerably in decisions made as result of output evaluation. Such decisions need to be made thoughtfully. Keeping in view they do not bring any difficulty and harm to anybody.

Objective Decisions

Decisions as a result of due deliberations and careful consideration of factors and forces pertinent in the issues or the problem to be solved are termed as objective decisions.

Subjective Decisions

Those decisions made in an organisation without conscious mental effort are called subjective decisions.

Programme or Routine Decisions

Decisions are those which do not require much deliberation and are repetitive in nature, in that on the occurrence of a particular situation a routine procedure is usually determined for solving it. Traditionally this type of decision has been handled through established rules, policies and standard operating procedures.

Non-programmed Decisions

These decisions traditionally have been handled primarily through general problem-solving processes—judgement, intention and hunch methods and creativity.

Organisational and Personal Decisions

Personal decisions are those which an executive makes in his individual capacity and not as a member of the organisation. There may be occasions, when he makes choices, involving his own actions. No delegation is possible in case of personal decisions.

Strategic Decisions (Financial, Production, Sale and Personnel)

These are of paramount importance to an organisation's long-range character: financial decisions involving large investment or expenditure and concerned with capital structure, credit terms, amount of working capital, securing new funds, credit terms, payment of dividends, cost of operation and liquidations; production decision relating to the volume of output, size of the plant, location of the plant, method of production, purchasing practice, wage payment; sale decisions concerned with determination of market, location of sales office, packing, price, advertising, sale promotional activities and marketing research; personnel decisions involving source of labour supply, selection techniques, recruitment policies, training, job analysis, promotions, evaluations and retirement.

Individual and Group Decisions

The decisions by an individual manager managed by the owner manager many be termed as individual decisions.

The group decisions suggest the pooling and combining of contributions by several thinkings-judgements. This is also called as participative decision making.

Emergency Decisions

Often on-the-spot, quick decisions, for problems as for instance, strikes, raw material hold-ups cancellation of a contract by a big customer, sudden sales resistance or controversy over new product and other unpredictable matters may be described as emergency decisions.

Characteristics of programmed and non-programmed decisions

	Programmed	*Non-programmed*
1.	Problems are routine and repetitive.	Problems are unique and novel.
2.	Solutions offered in accordance with some habit, rule or procedure.	There are no pre-established, policies or practice to rely on. Each situation is different and needs a creative solution.
3.	The conditions for programmed decisions are highly certain.	The conditions for non-programmed decisions are uncertain.
4.	Made by lower level people.	Top management responsibility.

DECISION MAKING CONDITIONS

Depending on the amount and quality of information available the decisions are made with one of three possible conditions: certainly, risk and uncertainty.

◄········ Increase knowledge

complete knowledge	certainty risk uncertainty Decrease knowledge	Incomplete knowledge

Decisions under Conditions of Certainty

Under conditions of certainty, the manager has enough information to be able to closely predict the outcome of various choices among alternatives. These decisions are simple and will maximise the desired outcome, e.g., if the manager decides to have a meeting with the subordinate in the afternoon, the chances are good that the subordinate will attend the meeting. Sometimes decisions made under conditions of certainty are highly complex, such as the scheduling of a number of different machines and products to be manufactured and assembled. In those situations complex mathematical models, such as linear programming, can be used.

Decisions under Conditions of Risk

Most of the manager's decisions are risk decisions, that is, some information is available, but it is insufficient to answer all questions about the outcome.

Decisions under Conditions of Uncertainty

Predictions of the future are never infallible, but under conditions of uncertainty the probabilities attached to the available alternatives are even less well known than under conditions of risk, e.g., it may be impossible to predict precisely how valuable a new price of equipment will be before it is installed.

Rational Decision Making

The term rationality implies a consistent and value maximising choice within certain limits. It means that the decision maker as an economic being tries to select the best alternative for achieving the optimum solution to a problem.

The decision making process is based on certain assumptions.

Decision making is a goal-oriented process

According to the rational economic model, the decision maker has a clear, well-defined goal that he is trying to maximise.

All choices are known

It is assumed that in a given decision situation, the decision maker can list (a) all the relevant criteria, (b) all the feasible alternatives, and (c) the consequences for each alternative.

Order of preference

It is assumed that the decision maker can rank all consequences according to preference and to select the alternative which has the preferred consequence.

Maximum advantage

The decision maker has the freedom to choose the alternative that best optimises the decisions. In other words, he would select that alternative which would maximise his satisfaction.

Rationality is an ideal and can be really achieved in an organisation. Many factors given below intervene with being perfectly rational:

a) Impossible to state the problem accurately.
b) Not fully aware of problems.
c) Imperfect knowledge.
d) Limited time and resources.
e) Cognitive limits.
f) Politics.

Administrative Model Decision Making

This model is proposed by Harbert A. Simon and refined by Richard Cyert and James March, which is to explain the decision making behaviour of individuals and organisations

According to Simon, people have only a limited, simplified view of problems confronting them because of certain reasons:

1) They do not have full information about the problem.
2) They do not possess knowledge of all the possible alternative solution to the problems and their consequences.
3) They do not have the ability to process competitive environmental and technical information.
4) They do not have sufficient time and resources to conduct an exhaustive search for an alternative solution to the problem.

This human and organisational limit makes it impossible for people to make perfectly rational decisions. There are always boundaries to rationality in an organisation.

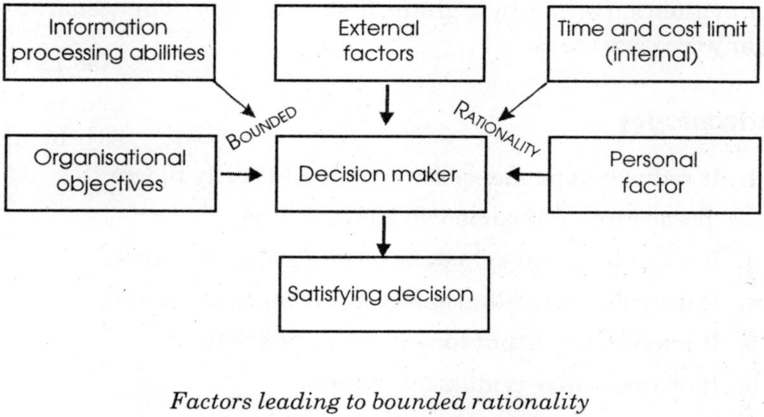

Factors leading to bounded rationality

TECHNIQUES IN DECISION MAKING

Problem Identification

The first step in a decision process is the identification of the accurate problem. At this stage it is necessary for the executives to collect (i) historical data, (ii) Planning of data, (iii) critical opinions, and (iv) newspaper information.

Identification of Alternatives

In order to develop alternatives a manager may employ four techniques.

i) Brainstorming

This is a technique designed to stimulate people to develop alternatives during the planning and decision making process. It encourages the sharing of ideas in a setting free of the interruptions and risks of immediate evolution and dimensions. To conduct a brainstorming session, the group is informed about the problem and asked to generate as many solutions as possible within a specified period of time. All ideas are recorded for evaluation either by a group or the manager. This generate many creative ideas.

Advantages

1. It reduces dependence on a single authority figure.
2. It encourages the open sharing of ideas.
3. It stimulates participation among group members.
4. It provides individual safety in a competitive group.
5. It maximises output for a short period of time.
6. It ensure a non-evaluative climate.
7. It tends to be enjoyable and stimulating.

ii) Synectics

The Greek word synectic means "the joining together of different and apparently irrelevant elements". The synectic techniques designed to develop creative ideas attempts to integrate diverse individuals into a problem-stating, problem-solving group. The technique gets people to focus on developing a single insightful solution and includes developing, evaluating and criticising ideas. Synectics is based on the assumption that a person is divided into two parts. The first part is concerned about safety and analytical, suspicious, logical and cautious, and thus inhibits experimentation and creativity. The second part strives towards learning and is impulsive and sensation seeking.

The synectic technique includes the following steps:

1. *Problem statement and background information stage:* The leader presents background information on the problem and goals associated with an ideal solution.
2. *Goalwishing stage:* Group members are encouraged to wish for anything that comes to mind that could address the problem.
3. *Execution stage:* Participants are asked to forget about a specific problem. They are asked to generate ideas about somewhat unrelated areas that eventually might be related to the problem at hand.
4. *Force for stage:* Participants take ideas from the execution stage and force them to fit the initial problem.
5. *Itemised response stage:* The group picks one of the ideas generated during the force-fit stage and pursues it further. All the positive ideas have been explored.

The outcome of the synectic process is a single unique plan or decision that has undergone considerable evaluation. The process tends to produce innovative ideas.

Although the synectic approach can be quite useful for creative planning and decision making, its cost is high. Further, it produces only one potential solution to a problem. If that solution turns out to be enviable, the problem remains and the process has failed.

Nominal group

The nominal group consists of people knowledgeable on the issue to be decided, who are in the same physical location and who are aware of each other but who do not directly interact while they are working together the step involved are:

1. The manager brings the group together and outlines the problem.
2. Each member of the group generates a number of ideas in writing.
3. Each member then presents a single idea at a time to the entire group. The ideas are written on a blackboard or on large pieces of paper and discussed for clarification.
4. The round robin continues with members adding to the ideas.
5. When no further ideas emerge, or when the manager feels the process has gone far enough, each member votes on the ideas, again in writing.
6. The final decision is the summed outcome of the individual votes but the manager is free to accept or reject it.

Delphi technique

The Delphi technique, named after the oracle at Delphi in ancient Greece, involves using the creative ideas of a group of people knowledgeable about the issue at hand, who work anonymously to solve the problems presented. The general process follows:

1. A panel of people who are knowledgeable about a particular problem selected, members from both inside and outside the organisation, they never meet and may or may not known each other.

2. A questionnaire about the problem to be solved is sent to each member and asked to make anonymous suggestions. These suggestions are pooled and a feedback report is developed.
3. The feedback report and a more advanced, second stage questionnaire are sent back to the panel members.
4. Each panel member independently evaluates the feedback report, votes on the priority of the ideas contained in it, and generates new idea based on it.
5. The process is repeated until a consensus is reached or until the manager feels that sufficient information has been received to make a decision.
6. A final summary feedback report is developed and sent back to the panel members.

SELECTION OF THE BEST ALTERNATIVES

Peter Drucker has offered the following four criteria for making the right choice among available alternatives:

1. Risk
2. Economy of effort
3. Timing
4. Limitation of resources

Groups as Decision Makers

Group decision making is different in process and outcome from the decision making done by individuals in the following ways:

Conformity

The forces that promote conformity within the group are the attitudes, beliefs, emotions which most of the members of the group have in common.

Group think

Group think is an extreme form of consensus in which the groups thinks as a unit rather than as a collection of individuals.

Superiority

Members drawn from different disciplines can bring a greater amount of information and expertise to bear on a problem to generate more creative alternative solutions and make it more likely that the solution would be understood, accepted and implemented.

Risky shift

The average risk-taking score tends to be higher in groups. There is considerable evidence to show that in some situations, groups make riskier decisions than individuals.

Advantages and Disadvantages of Group Decision Making

	Advantages	*Disadvantages*
1.	A group has more information than an individual. Members from different fields can provide more knowledge about a problem.	Groups are notorious time wasters.
2.	A group generates a greater number of alternatives.	Groups create pressures toward conformity.
3.	Participation in group decisions increases the acceptance and commitment on the part of the people.	Presence of some powerful and influential members prevent other members from participating freely.
4.	People understand the decision better because they have seen and heard it develop.	It may be very costly to secure the participation from several individuals.
5.	Interaction between individuals with varied view-points leads to greater creativity.	The group consists of several members and hence it is easy to pass the buck and avoid responsibility.
6.	Groups may also be able to capitalise on individual talents.	Disagreement over arriving at a decision may lead to conflict, recestment and ill-feelings between group members.

Ways to Improve Decision Making

There are many ways to improve the decision making process. One is simply to gain knowledge of the different tools available which involve an increase in one's vocabulary.

Another way to improve decision making is by practice. Other ways of improving decision making are (1) Education and training, (2) Use of mathematical and similar aids, and (3) Use of group techniques.

Education and training

Training is a broad process that involves the learning of concepts, skills, rules and attitudes. Education and training from classrooms and books can lead to more effective decision making if the decision maker, applies the acquired knowledge. A characteristic of the effective manager is the ability to learn from almost every life experience and from other people's expertise.

Learning on the job involves careful evaluations of the results of one's decisions.

Use of mathematical and similar aids

Many different tools have been developed to help improve the decision making process. Some of the tools are qualitative, others are numerical or mathematical. Qualitative tools consist of knowledge of individual motivation, of group dynamics and of organisational structure.

Some of the mathematical tools that are of direct help in decision making, planning and controlling are linear programming, budgeting, break-even analysis and perform-ance ratios. These tools range from relatively simple to relatively complex in nature.

Effective decision making with subordinates and others

Much of the manager's time is spent working with other people and much of what a manager does is therefore influenced by others. Most decisions involve others, and many are arrived at through some sort of group process. Thus the decision making process may involve the manager making the decision alone, with selected subordinates, with subordinates as a group or with a group composed of both immediate subordinates and others.

5

Communication Skills for Effective Supervision

The basic managerial functions—organising, planning, directing, controlling—have their lifetimes firmly rooted in the organisational heartbeat of communication only. Peter Drucker pointed out that the manager's effectiveness depends on his ability to listen and read, to speak and write.

Communication is an artery of an organisation through which instructions, orders and decisions of the management flow down to the lower levels. It also conducts upward the pulse of workforce. Basically communication refers to the process of passing information and understanding from one person to another. It involves the exchange of facts, ideas, opinions or emotions by two or more individuals. Communications bridge meaning between people.

The supervisor represents the link that conveys how plans, policies and direction coming from above have to be interpreted into meaningful goals and direction of his own people, and transmit the feedback from employees to the top management.

IMPORTANCE OF COMMUNICATION

Communication is important to all managers. According to Bernard, the first executive function is to develop and maintain a system of communication. In fact, a large part of the manager's time is spent in some form of communication—writing, reading, speaking or listening. Communication is the means by which he persuades, informs, motivates and leads employees towards organisational goals.

Communication is important in management because:

1) Of basis of action.
2) It facilitates planning.
3) It helps in decision-making.
4) It is a means of coordination.
5) It improves the relationships.
6) It improves motivation and morale.

Purpose of Communication

According to Kaohtz and Weihrich (1980), the purpose of communication in an enterprise is to effect change—to influence action towards the welfare and internal functioning of the enterprises, because it integrates managerial functions.

Communication is especially needed to:

1. Establish and disseminate goals of the enterprise.
2. Develop plan for their achievement.
3. Organise human and other resources, in the most effective and efficient way.
4. Select, develop and preappraise members of the organisation.
5. Lead, direct, motivate and create interest in which people to want to contribute
6. Control performance.

Communication also relates an enterprise to its external environment, like needs of customers, availability of suppliers, claims of stockholders, regulations of Government and concerns of a community.

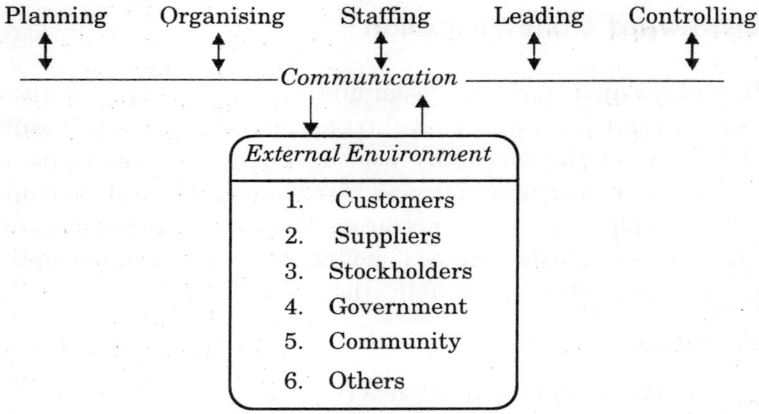

The purpose and functions of communication

Elements of Communication

The major elements of communication process are:

1. *Gestures*: Physical action, facial expression and non-verbal.
2. *Spoken words*: Syntax, verbal symbols and voice inflection.
3. *Written words*: Syntax, word symbols premiership and time elements.
4. *The emotional or conscious state* of sender and receiver or listener.

During the exchange the readiness of the listener or reader to receive a message, trust, respect and psychological climate is important.

Communication Flow in an Organisation

In an effective organisation, communication flows in various directions, downward, upward, horizontal and diagonal. The supervisor should adopt all types of communication flows for effective work of the organisation.

Downward Communication

It is also called "top-down" communication. The flows of information right from upper level (superior) to lower levels (subordinates) of the hierarchy pass through a formal chain of command. The primary purpose is to transmit information and instruct employees in the performance of job. This includes job instructions, official memos, policy statements, procedures, manuals, sanctions, and publications.

Limitations

1. Distortion or modification of the message.
2. Status and reliability of the source.
3. Lack of understanding by subordinates.
4. Sequence observations in the presentation of the message.
5. Timing.

Upward Communication

It is called "Bottom-up" communication. The flow of information is from the subordinates to the superiors in the organisation. It provides a feedback on how well things are going. The upward communication usually consists of (1) suggestions for improvement, (ii) requests for help or information, and (iii) expression of attitudes or feelings. The methods includes open-door policies, grievance procedures, participation and attitude surveys.

Limitations

a) Fear of distortion.
b) Status consideration.
c) Barriers.

Horizontal Communications

It is called as "Cross Communication" (lateral). It takes place between people on the same level of hierarchy. It promotes coordination and team work.

Diagonal Communication

It takes place between people who are neither in the same department nor in the same level of hierarchy. Consequently, this form of communication should be used carefully by observing two simple rules: (1) obtain permission from one's direct supervisor, or (ii) inform the direct supervisor before cross-communication.

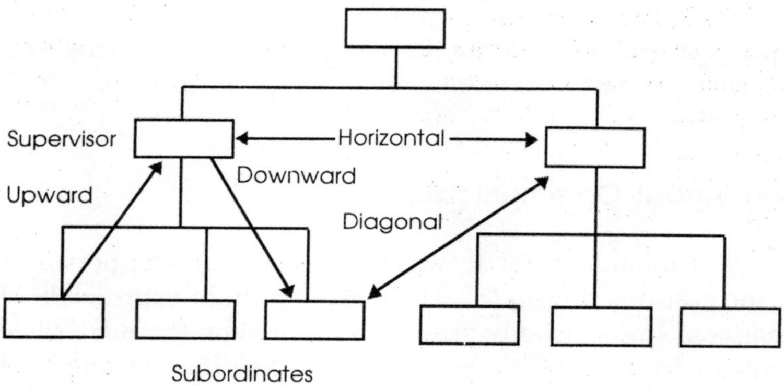

FORMS OF COMMUNICATION

Oral or Verbal Communication

Oral communication is face-to-face communication between individuals. It can also take place via telephone, public address system and other media. Studies have shown that oral communications are more effective than written communications in conveying feelings or in changing attitudes or beliefs. One advantage is its potential for speedy and complete interchange. When the time for communication is short and the message is somewhat abridged oral communication is generally used. However, messages are lengthy and to reach a large audience oral communication is not suitable.

Written Communication

It has several advantages:

1) It provides a record for referral and follow-up.
2) It is a means of providing identical messages, for large people.
3) Written communication is simpler.

The major limitation is that the sender does not know how or if the communication is received; feedback is late, and it is expensive.

Non-verbal Communication

People communicate by the way they look at another person or by the gestures they make. The most important expressions of emotional states usually are communicated on the non-verbal level. Andrew J. Dubrin has indicated the different modes of transmitting non-verbal messages.

Head, face and eye behaviour

A combination of head, face and eye contact provides the clearest indications of attitudes towards other people.

Posture

Learning toward another individual suggests that he is favourable towards messages.

Distance

Relatively close proximity shows friendlier and more understanding than people farther away.

Gesture

Positive attitudes are shown by frequent head movements.

Tone of the voice

Anger is often perceived when the source speaks loundly, quickly and with irregular inflection and clipped enunciation.

Environmental cues

Location, room colour, lighting and furniture arrangement can influence the receiving of a message.

Clothing, dress and appearance

Dress is often said to influence the appearance of power to others.

Use of time

A subtle mode of non-verbal communication in an organisation is the use of time. If we are late for a meeting we might be regarded as careless.

COMMUNICATION NETWORK

A number of one or two-way channels of communication build up into a network. The three important types of network can be identified in an organisation. According to Cohen (1985), the following are the chief networks:

Wheel

For straight forward communications this is a quick and effective network. From the personnel management point of view, its importance, i.e., in the advantageous position. 'A', i.e., as manager and four 'subordinates, he has to filter or modify communication between others. This puts him in a powerful leadership position.

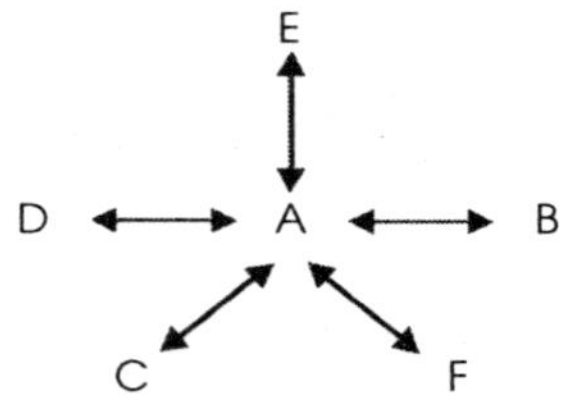

Circle

Both the risk of overloading and the leadership situation are eliminated in the circle network. However, this network is slow and unreliable or inefficient if any members are absent or inefficient. It is mainly used for the dissemination of information for further use.

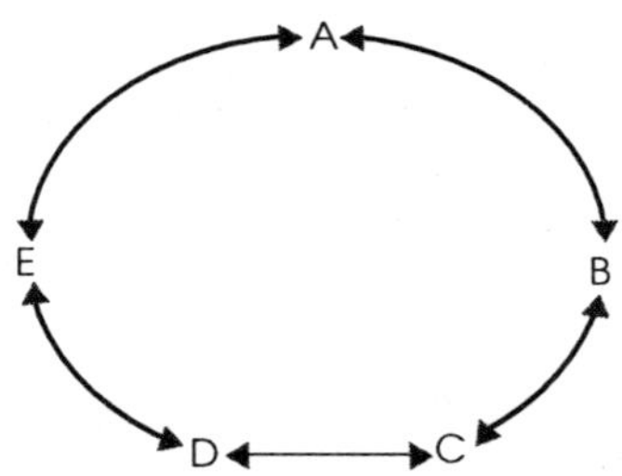

All-Channel Network

In this network, through communication between all members is facilitated and encouraged. It is very effective for a two-way communication and exchange of ideas as in a committee.

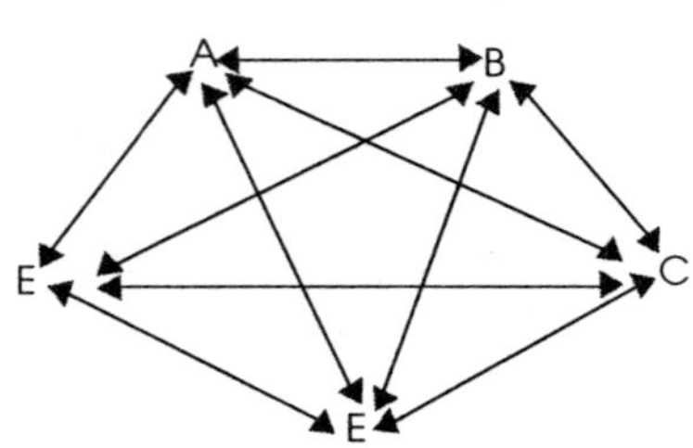

Requirements of Good Communication Network

a) Adequate channel size
b) Economy
c) Efficiency
d) Reliability

Use of Communication

Examples of typical activities of communication involved are:

Communication upward

a) Reports
b) Worksheets
c) Recommendation of solutions to problems
d) Past experience
e) Information transmission

Communication downward

a) Instructions and orders
b) Training
c) Advice
d) Transmitting information for any of the above
e) Informing subordinates

Communication sideways

a) Conference and meeting
b) Discussion of data and problem
c) Information on progress

According to Umasekaran (1989), five most common network communications are

1) Chain

```
A         B         C         D
0---------0---------0---------0
```

communication in an organisation hierarchy.

2) Wheel or star

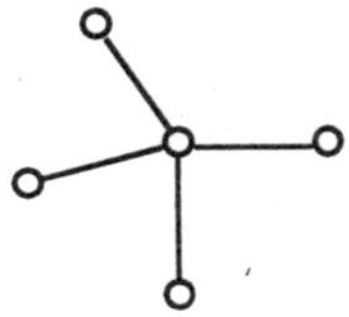

3) Circle

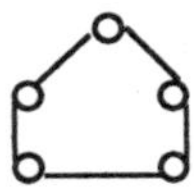

4) All channel

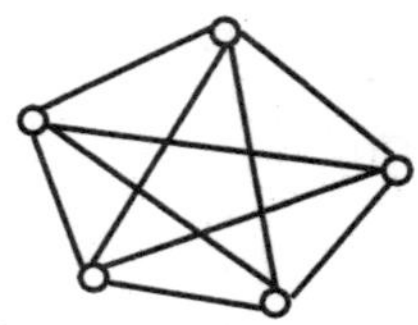

5) Inverse *Y* network

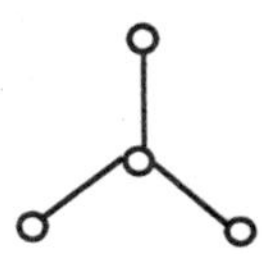

where two people report to a boss, who has two levels above.

Communication Skills

The supervisor should have five communication skills. Two of these are encoding skills in writing and speaking and two are decoding skills in reading and listening; the fifth is crucial in both encoding and decoding skill thought or reasoning.

From the organisation point of view, communication skills include the supervisor's (manager) ability to plan a communication strategy, his ability to write, speak and listen to the message, and analyse the feedback.

Improving Oral Communication

The supervisor spends most of the his time in communicating with his subordinates. An effective oral communicator should be able to achieve comprehension, understanding, perceived utility and validity and leave a lasting impression of the message in the mind of the listener.

Clear objectives

The supervisor should have clear objectives and use appropriate language for communicating message with his subordinates.

Good relationship with subordinates

The supervisor's good report, positive attitude, pleasing personalities, language compatibility, close contact, the ability to listen and analyse problems are perceived to credibly influence reception, interpretation and response to a message.

Effective delivery

The supervisor can follow some simple rules for effective communication, viz., talk clearly, loudly, slowly, sweetly and the truth. If possible, clarify and repeat the key ideas.

Written Communication

Common problems in written communication are that writers omit the conclusion, are too wordy, use poor grammar and incorrect spelling. The following guidelines may improve communication skills:

a) Use simple words and phrases.
b) Use short sentences and paragraphs.
c) Use familiar words.
d) Use pronouns and active verbs.
e) Avoid unnecessary words.

Informal Communication

Informal communication channels exist outside the official network and develop because the spontaneous interaction between people work in an organisation. The common informal communication is known as the grapevine (rumour mill). There is no prescribed direction of flow of messages nor is there any ready available means for verifying them. The grapevine can carry erroneous messages as well as accurate ones. According to Prof. Keith Davis, grapevines are a natural and inevitable part of the organisational life. The manager's (supervisors) job is to understand the nature of the grapevine, accept it, prune the distorted branches and cultivate the good ones. He must make a constructive use of the grapevine and use it to supplement formal communication.

Good Communication: Ten Commandments

Communication is the basis of managerial work. It is, therefore, necessary for a supervisor to study its many aspects and educate the staff about the importance of good communication.

The following ten commandments may help a supervisor to improve his communicating skills.

1. *Clarity:* Think and plan before communicating. Be clear about what you want to communicate. The more systematically a problem or idea is analysed, the clearer it becomes.
2. *Purpose:* State the purpose of each communication. Obtain information, imitate action, change another person's attitude. Don't try to accomplish too much with each communication. The sharper the focus of your message the greater chances of success.
3) *Physical and human setting:* Be sensitive to the total communication. The supervisor should analyse the physical setting and social culture governing work relationship before issuing orders or directives. The communication should also conform to the expectations of subordinates, and take their past practice and customs also into consideration.

4. *Participation:* Invite others to participate in planning a communication which helps in additional insight and objectivity of message. Moreover, those who have helped in planning communication will give their active support.
5. *Word choice and body language:* Select simple words and use them carefully so that they do not take on different meanings to different people. The body of the language should support the written communication.
6. *Empathy:* When the supervisors are empathetic, they create a climate that encourages the subordinates to communicate often and honestly with them.
7. *Actions*: A supervisor should support communication through good supervisory efforts, clear assignment of duties, fair rewards for effort, sound policy enforcement, etc. Such parties serve to communicate more than all the gifts of oratory.
8. *Use of feedback*: The supervisor should provide feedback which provides an open channel, so that he can check how the messages are being perceived. He should create an environment that encourages feedback.
9. *Communicate for tomorrow as well as today:* Communication should be planned with the past in mind so as to support the organisation policies consistency. They must take into account the short-run interest of the organisation.
10. *Be a good listener*: Listening is the one of most important, most difficult and most neglected skills in communication. Often managers are not prepared to listen to what subordinates say. To improve listening we need to become more than passive receivers. Keith Davis has developed 10 guidelines to effective listening: (a) stop talking, (b) put the talker at ease, (c) show the talker that you want to listen, (d) remove distraction, (e) empathise with the talker (f) be patient (g) curb your temper, (h) go easy on argument and criticism, (i) stop talking.

Barriers and Breakdown in Communications

Communication takes place between individuals who have different background and personalities. Age, race, sex, education, family background and host of other differences influences our behaviour in organisations. Besides, there are many organisational barriers impending the free flow of information between individuals. There are many other external barriers that impede the smooth flow of messages.

According to Venkataiah and Rao (1993), the barriers are:

1) *Semitic Barriers*

Many of our communication problems are semitic in nature; as the same word may convey a different meaning to different people. When two individuals attach different meanings to a word, a breakdown in communication can occur.

2) *Interpersonal Barriers*

   a) Some people cannot use words and their personality effectively.
   b) Filtering of information becomes a barrier to effective communication.
   c) All supervisory efforts will fail to motivate subordinates if they believe that he is not credible and trustworthy.
   d) A supervisor can often be near but is inattentive.
   e) Perceptual differences—past experience, belief, values, emotion, also affect each person's perception.
   f) Jealousy also plays an important role in reducing communication effectiveness.

3) *Structural Barriers*

   a) Hierarchical level—messages likely to be delayed.
   b) Status relationship—superiors are reluctant to discuss important problems with subordinates.
   c) Specialisation—loyal to departments.

Different functions, special interests, job jargon, community feeling, tunnel vision, parts mentality and section interest also prevent employees to listen to others.

According to Rao and Narayana (1996), the barriers may be due to the following:

1. *Filtering:* Sometimes the information is filtered by the manager himself, hiding some meaning and discussing in such a fashion as appealing to the employee.
2. *Selective perception:* In communication, the process generally involves selective perception, i.e., the supervisor perceives the messages based on the organisational requirements, the needs and background of the employees.
3. *Emotions:* How the receiver feels at the time of the receipt of information influences effectively, how he interprets the information. Extreme emotion and jubilation or depression are quite likely to hinder the effectiveness of communication.
4. *Language:* Language by its every nature is incomplete and semantics create communication problems. In organisations, people come from different regions, different backgrounds and speak different languages.
5. *Information overload*: Managers are flooded with information from various corners. In this process, inevitably many of the messages are either overlooked or misinterpreted.
6. *Non-verbal cues*: Sometimes, non-verbal cues are inconsistent with the oral message and the receiver gets confused because lack of clarity of message.
7. *Time pressures:* Managers are often subjected to time pressures, because decisions must be made within the specified deadlines. Such time pressures can create communication problems.

Overcoming barriers

To make communication effective managers must attempt to remove the barriers. Though there are no prescribed techniques or ways of overcoming barriers, the following ways represents one way of overcoming barriers to communication.

1. *Regulate the flow of information:* A sound approach in management could be that incoming communication may be condensed or edited and arranged in the order of merit of what and when actions are to be taken.
2. *Feedback:* One easy way of overcoming barriers to communication is to have a feedback. The manager, immediately after communicating a message, can ask the receiver's response.
3. *Simplify language:* For effective communication, the managers should try to avoid complicated jargons, and use simple language that a subordinate understands.
4. *Listen carefully:* Listening is active and intellectual process, good listening removes communication barriers.
5. *Constrain emotions:* When the either subordinate or the manager is mentally upset, over an issue, they are quite likely to misconstrue the message. In such a situation defer the communication until you have regained composive and coolness.
6. *Watch non-verbal cues:* In the case of oral communication, a manager should carefully observe the non-verbal cues of subordinates towards the message. He should be careful dealing with the grapevine because it can carry damaging rumours that adversely effect the effectiveness of communication.

6

Coordination and Cooperation in Supervision

Coordination is the integration, synchronisation or orderly pattern of individual and group effort to achieve organisational objectives. Coordination affects the people, groups, organisational units and all activities within every enterprise. Lack of coordination causes tremendous waste of time, effort and money.

Some of the traditional management scholar's like Foyal, Mooney, Tead, Urwick, Breach, Gullick and Allen consider coordination as a "separate function of management". They felt that when all the management functions are performed effectively, coordination was achieved automatically. Coordination permeates the entire process of management. In fact, coordination is a common thread running through all the management functions.

DEFINITIONS

> Coordination deals with synchronising and unifying the actions of a group of people. A coordinated operation is one in which the activities of the employee are harmonious, dovetailed and integrated towards common objectives.
>
> —*W.H. Newman,* (1956).

> Coordination is an act necessary to harmonise all the activities of a concern so as to facilitate its working and its success.
> —*Henry Foyal*

According to J.D. Mooney, coordination is an orderly arrangement of group effort to provide unity of action in pursuit of a common goal.

a) *Group effect:* Organisation is not a haphazard collection of people, materials, machines, equipment and other financial and physical resources. The financial, human and technical resources are properly organised and coordinated. Coordination transcends and permeates all managerial functions. It is the orderly synchronisation of efforts of the subordinates to provide the proper amount of timing and quality of execution, so that their united efforts lead to stated objectives of organisation.

b) *Unit of action:* Coordination applies to the group effort, not individual effort. It stresses the unity of effort and unity of action. It is an ongoing process where managers develop an integrated and orderly synchronisation of group effort among their subordinates and try to attain unity of effort in pursuit of same common objectives.

c) *Common purpose:* Effective management is *sine qua non* of good management. Coordination is not a one-shot deal, it is a never-ending process of ensuing achievement. If organisational goals effectively. Coordination involves the reciprocal relationship i.e., willingness to take and give among the people and activities concerned. Individuals having own perception, attitude, beliefs values etc. which create conflict. The demand of coordination of efforts to achieve common goals.

Without coordination, individuals and departments would lose sight of their roles within the organisations. The need of coordination depends upon the nature and communication requirements of the tasks performed and the degree of interdependence of the various sub-units performing them.

According to James D. Thompson, there are three varieties of interdependence among organisational units:

i) *People's interdependence:* This exists when organisational units do not depend upon one another to carry their day-to-day work but do depend on the adequate performance of each unity for ultimate survival. Each part renders a separate contribution to the whole and is supported by the whole, e.g., bank; court.
ii) *Sequential interdependence:* One organisational unit must act before the next one, e.g., fertiliser or insecticide organisation
iii) *Reciprocal interdependence:* This involves give and take relationships between such-units.

The need for coordination of organisational activities is the least with pealed interdependence, greater with sequential interdependence, and greatest with reciprocal interdependence. As the need for coordination increases so does the difficulty of achieving effectively. Similarly, with increased specialisation, the more difficult for managers to coordinate the specialised activities of the different units.

Paul R. Lawrence and Jay W. Lorsch have identified four types of differences in attitude and working style that tend to arise among the various individuals and departments in organisations. These differences will complicate the task of effective coordination.

1. *Differences in orientation toward particular goals:* Members of different departments develop their own view about how best to advance the interest of the organisation:
2. *Differences in time orientation:* Some members of an organisation, such as the production manager, will be more concerned with problems that have to be solved immediately or within a short period of time, whereas the research and development team may take years to solve.

3. *Difference in interpersonal orientation:* In some organisational, activities such as production decision and communication, are quick whereas in R&D, the style of communication may be easygoing.
4. *Difference in formal structures:* Each sub-unit in the organisation may have different methods and standards for evaluating progress towards objectives and for rewarding employees.

Approaches to Achieving Effective Coordination

Communication is the key to effective coordination. Coordination is directly dependent upon the acquisition, transmission and processing of information. Therefore, coordination is essentially an information processing task. Three approaches are:

i) *Basis management techniques:* The managerial hierarchy plans and gives general direction to activities and rules and procedures to guide them. Organisations with relatively modest coordination requirements may not need more than this.

ii) *Increase coordination potential:* It is necessary when the organisation's various sub-units become more interdependent or expands in the size of functions. Then the quantity of information necessary to achieve its objectives increases and its coordination potential must also be increased.

iii) *Reduce the need for coordination:* In this approach instead of increasing coordination potential, it reduces the coordination need. In some situations it is not efficient to develop additional ways of coordinating, and managers may decide to reduce the need for coordination by providing more resources to organisational sub-unit or by regrouping sub units so that the tasks are self-contained.

Approach I

Basic Managment Techniques

1. Rules and programme
2. Managerial hierarchy
3. Goal setting

Approach II

Increased Coordination Potential

4. Investment in vertical information system
5. Creation of lateral relations

Approach III

Reduced Need for Coordination

6. Creation of stock resources
7. Creation of self-contained tasks

Three approaches to effective coordination methods for managers

BASIC FEATURES OF COORDINATION

1. If the subdivision of work is inescapable coordination becomes mandatory.
2. Coordination is a process of achieving integration among different organisational units.
3. The idea that coordination is a fixed entity, is present in all organisations but in varying degree.
4. Undue confusion is a symptom of poor coordination.
5. Unity of effort is the heart of the coordination problem.
6. The chief objective of coordination is a common purpose.
7. Coordination cannot be achieved automatically, it must be won by intelligent, vigorous, persistent and organised effort.

IMPORTANCE OF COORDINATION

Coordination is the epitome of management. As Bernard has pointed out, "coordination is a crucial factor in the survival of any enterprise". The need for coordination, as pointed out by Brech, "arises from the diversity of tasks to be undertaken and the persons to carry them out". If emerges as soon as the operation begins, to be multiple or complex by reason of the fact that more persons are concerned with it. Coordination is essential for:

1. Resolving conflicts between line and staff, inter-departmental infra-departmental conflicts and restoring harmony in operations.
2. Resulting in the accomplishment of organisational goals.
3. Helping in increase the effectiveness of management.

Henry Foyal, the father of modern management, has pointed out:

1. Each department works in harmony with the rest.
2. In each department divisions and subdivisions are precisely informed as to their share in the task.
3. The working schedule of the various departments and subdivisions there of is constantly attended to in circumstances.

PRINCIPLES OF COORDINATION

Coordination is the continuous and dynamic process and emphasises unity of effort to achieve the desired objectives. Coordination is essentially the managerial responsibility. Mary Parker Fullett (1940) has spelt various principles of coordination.

Principle of Direct Contact

1. Coordination can be achieved by direct contact among the responsible· people concerned. Such personal contacts bring about an agreement on methods, actions and ultimate achievement of objectives.

2. *Early stages:* Coordination should start from the very beginning of the planning process. At the time of policy formulation and objective setting, a combination can be sought from organisational participants.
3. *Reciprocal relationships:* All factors in a situation are reciprocally related. In other words, all the parts influence and are influenced by other parts.
4. *Principle of continuity:* Coordination is neverceasing and a never ending exercise of managers. It is something which must go on all the time in the organisation.
5. *Principle of self-coordination:* This principle is emphasised by Brown. According to this principle, when a particular department affects other functions or departments, it is in turn affected by other departments or functions. However, if other departments are modified in such a fashion that this affects a particular department favourably then self-coordination is achieved.

How Coordination Helps to Increase the Effectiveness of Management

Coordination helps to increase the effectiveness of management in the following ways:

1. Coordination pulls all the functions and activities together. In the absence of coordination the energies, resources, skills, and intelligence of people, material and financial resources cannot follow a specification direction.
2. Coordination brings unity of action and direction. It resolves effectively the dangerous conflict between individuals and organisational goals.
3. Activities are divided and subdivided in organisations, and such differentiation requires effective interaction of activities. The integration is brought about by coordinations in terms of fusion among differentiated work units and authority centres.

4. Modern organisations are considered as an open system. These open systems are characterised by information flows, resources flows and flows of activities. Coordination ensures the smooth flow of activities. Coordination ensures the smooth flow of resources into productive units and brings the required quality of output.

Techniques to Achieve Coordination

Supervisors use a variety of techniques for achieving the coordination. The main ones includes:

1) *Coordination by rules or procedures*: For coordinating the routine, recurring activities, rules and procedures are helpful. Rules and procedures specify in detail and ahead of time, what course of action the subordinates should take if some situation should arise.
2) *Coordination by targets or goals:* Most of the supervisors assign specific goals/targets to their subordinates to facilitate coordination.
3) *Coordination through hierarchy:* Rules, regulations and procedures as well as goals apart, supervisors also use the chain of command to achieve coordination.
4) *Coordination through departmentalisation:* Departmentalisation also serves as a technique to bring about effective coordination. Some form of departmentalisation with coordination works better than others.
5) *Using staff assistant for coordination:* To make his job of coordinating easier, a supervisor may hire an assistant. When subordinates bring a problem to him, the assistant can compile the information on the problem and provide alternative solutions. This increases the supervisor's ability to handle problems and coordinate the work of his subordinates.
6) *Using a liaison for coordination:* In some big organisations, where the contacts between two departments are high, many managers appoint a special liaison person to facilitiate coordination.

7) *Using a committee of coordination:* Another sound technique of coordination is to form committees for understanding various functions and problems. Committees are increasingly useful for coordinating, planning and execution of programmes and controlling various activities. These days supervisors achieve the coordination by creating an interdepartmental committee, task forces and teams. Committee also establish face-to-face contact and personal relationships and promote voluntary cooperation.

8) *Using independent integrators for coordination*: An independent integrator's job is to coordinate the activities of several interdependent departments. Using independent integrators for achieving coordination was proved to be useful in high-technology companies, where the work of several independent departments are coordinated especially under rapidly changing condition and business environment.

9) *Conference:* Conferences at regular intervals also ensure better coordination. Conferences provide adequate platform for discussion of various problems being encountered by different departments. Free and candid discussions reveal coordination problems, if any, and pave the way for a smooth coordination and ultimate success of the enterprise.

10) *The techniques of communication:* The welldesigned communication is an artery through which the decisions flow from top to bottom and reports flow from bottom to top. Any communication gap has a high probability of distributing the continuity of operation and may be at the cost of coordination.

11) *Miscellaneous:* Other coordinating techniques are grouping similar activities, reorganisation of departments, cross-functioning of the departments, project management, planning techniques, creation of certain staff positions, organisation hierarchy, periodical staff meeting, etc.

CONSTRAINTS IN COORDINATION

For the success of any organisation, coordination must exist between different departments, groups and activities. Unfortunately, there are some limitations to the degree of coordination that can be achieved in any organisation. Some of the constraints for effective coordination arise from the following:

1. The uncertain future poses a threatening challenge to coordination. Natural phenomena like rains and crops, floods and certain abnormal changes in the behaviour of individuals and groups in organisations are examples of an uncertain future.
2. The knowledge, experience, character and wisdom of the supervisors and their confirmed and conflicting objectives and ideas also act as a constraint for effective coordination.
3. Lack of administrative skills and lack of adequate knowledge of necessary techniques on the part of supervisors also limit the degree of coordination in an organisation.
4. Lack of orderly method of developing and adopting new ideas and programmes is a constraint.
5. A vast number of variables involved in the incompleteness of human knowledge, particularly with regard to man and his life also limit the degree of coordination.

COORDINATION VS COOPERATION

The terms coordination and cooperation are widely used but mostly confused. Cooperation indicates the willingness of people to help each other. Coordination is a much more inclusive concept; it requires more than mere desire and willingness on the part of participants. Cooperation is a necessary adjunct to proper coordination; for without cooperation the question of coordination does not arise. Coordination is organisational process where cooperation is purely individual and personal.

The chief points of distinction between coordination and cooperation are captured hereunder.

Status

Coordination is a necessary function of management. It is actually the epitome of all management functions. Coordination is vital to carry out all management functions successfully.

Cooperation on the other hand does not enjoy the status of a separate function management. It is more of an attitude of an individual and group than anything else. It, however, is essential for successful coordination of different parts.

Deliberate Action

Coordination is the deliberate and intentional effort of the manager. Cooperation on the other hand, is voluntary. Management can function even without cooperation, but ceases to function without coordination.

Necessity

The nature of work in every organisation is such that it needs to be divided and integrated. Coordination of all interdependent activities is of utmost importance for the success of the organisation. Coordination is therefore the inevitable necessity.

Cooperation, on the other hand, does not arise out of any limitations of structure and organisations. The individuals must learn to cooperate with each other even though their activities are least related.

Broader Concept

Cooperation is necessary for achieving successful coordination. Therefore, coordination is the broader concept. Sometimes cooperation between individual members may exist and coordination between departments may not exist. The organisation fails to deliver the goods required because of the lack of coordination.

To be effective an organisation requires both cooperation and coordination. As Herbert Simon points out, cooperation will usually be ineffective (it will not reach its goal) whatever the intention of participants, in the absence of coordination.

Thus, the supervisors must initiate cooperation among individuals and coordination between departments for effective functioning of an organisation.

REFERENCES

Aggarwala, D.V., 1984, *Management principles, practices and techniques,* Deep and Deep publications, New Delhi.

Cohen, Gerald.J., 1985, *The nature of management,* Graham and Tretman.

Eckels.W.Robert, R.L. Chamscheel and Sarchet Berbard R., 1974, *Essentials of management for first-line supervision,* John Wiley and Sons, Inc., New York.

Halloram, Jack and G.L. Frunzi, 1988, *Supervision, The art of management,* Practice-Hall International Inc.

Hersey, Paul and Kenneth.R.Blanchorrd 1992, *Management of organisational behaviour—utility of human resources,* prentice Hall of India Pvt.Ltd., New Delhi.

Keentz, H and H. Weihrich, 1990,*Essentials of management,* McGraw-Hill Pub.Co, New York

Lester Bittel R., 1985, *What every supervisor should know, The basics of supervisory management,* Tata McGraw-Hill Pub.Co.Ltd., New Delhi.

Maheswari, B.L., 1980, *Decision styles and organisational effectiveness,* Vikas Pub. House Pvt. Ltd.

Rao, V.S.P. and P.S. Narayana, 1996, *Principles and practices of management,* Konark Pub. Pvt. Ltd., New Delhi.

Roy, M. Charles and Elson L. Charles, 1983, *Supervision,* The Drydon Press, Chicago.

Stener James A., 1984, *Management,* Prentice-Hall of India Pvt. Ltd.

Umashekaran, 1989, *Organisational behaviour—Text and* cases, Tata McGraw-Hill Pvt. Company Ltd.

Venkataiah, V and Surya Prakash Rao V., 1993, *Fundamentals of management, functions and behaviour,* Discovery Publication House, New Delhi.

Yull, Bruce, 1968, *Supervision principles and techniques,* George Allen and Unwin Ltd, London.

7

The Role of Supervision in Extension Administration

For many long years there was no clearcut distinction between the role of a supervisor and a worker, except that supervisors were loyal and capable workers who could be trusted by those in higher levels of management to share the burden of work. Their job was to keep the workers on task. They were placed in a position of having to cross the management labour-breach. Experience for a worker was essential for becoming a supervisor. It was assumed that supervisors must have done the work before they could supervise doing that work.

WHAT IS SUPERVISION?

Supervision is an art of directing the efforts or harnessing the energy of human beings to attain organisational goals/ objectives.

WHO IS A SUPERVISOR?

One who oversees the work of others is known as a supervisor. It is also termed as the power to command or the ability to dominate. The supervisor acts as a liaison agent between union and management. So he is called a catalyst or link person between management and workers or union. Categorisation of employees increases productivity in organisations.

What are the Good Qualities of a Supervisor?

1. Thoroughness—in work is very crucial
2. Fairness—Unbiased
3. Initiative—assuming responsibilities
4. Tactful—in tackling issues
5. Enthusiasm—eagerness and interest
6. Emotional control—exercising patience
7. Intelligent
8. Integrity
9. Loyal
10. Flexibility

What do Supervisors do?

Dowell and Wexley attempted to identify the primary dimensions of a first line supervisor's jobs, while their findings are slanted toward the supervisor's jobs in industry. But their findings can be used as a foundation for explaining the work of any kind, which include:

a) working with subordinates
b) organising the work of subordinates
c) work planning and scheduling
d) maintaining efficient quality of production
e) maintaining safe, clean work areas
f) maintaining equipment and machinery
g) compiling records and reports.

Supervisors who have little practical experience in the work they will supervise are not uncommon. But some areas of the technical work still require extensive hands of experience on the part of those appointed for supervision. The preparation of supervisors through formal training rather than practical experience, is still an issue in some circles, but many organisation leaders have accepted the fact that abilities in other things are also essential.

Workers Views on a Supervisor's Role

Historically, the supervisory role varied from one organisation to another. Many management authorities suggest that the role of a supervisor has slipped to something less than a management role, at least in the eyes of the worker. They push for an environment that would put supervisors sending them back into the management camp. Where a supervisor was a manager to the employee only half a century ago, he or she has now, by and large, become a buffer between management and union and worker. Like others, the supervisor's main function is to take the blows.

Some supervisors may be caught between workers who expect to be protected form higher management and management which holds supervisors responsible for the work that goes on in their areas. This conflict appears to be solved in organisations which place supervisors firmly in the realm of management with well defined jobs, a sense of responsibility for their workers and a voice in the decision-making process. They are considered a part of the management team, not enforces of management rules and regulations.

What is Supervisory Management?

It is a basic management form and the most important managerial activity of supervising others' work. These supervisors are meant to be masters with:

a) skills in dealing with management workers
b) technical skills—technical methods used
c) professional skills—competency
d) interpersonal skills—leading, directing and understanding people

e) administrative skills—activities involving direction
f) human relation skills—organisational behaviour
g) communication skills—art of communicating with others

Skills Needed by Supervisors

Level of Management		*Skills needed*	
Top	5%	60%	35%
Middle	20%	60%	20%
Supervisory	35%	60%	5%

Source: Charles *et al.* (1983) : 12

The broad roles of supervisors centre around the following dimensions and is supported by Koontz and Odenell (1984), Dahama and Bhatnagar (1984), Koontz and Weinrich (1990) and Benner (1983):

a) Clarifying organisational roles
b) Setting subordinate objectives
c) Planning
d) Controlling
e) Organising
f) Coordination
g) Directing
h) Review of work progress
i) Technical support
j) Span of control
k) Supply of service
k) Training

Role of Supervisors

Supervisors are to be found in every type of work organisation, that is to say, social and economic service to community, business organisations—pursuit of profit, social service organisation—hospitals and schools. They are also found in governmental organisations. But their functions vary with organisations associated, so it is difficult to clearly categorise their roles.

Most organisations have at least five levels: (a) Top management, (b) Chief executive, (c) Senior, (d) Middle and (e) Supervisory levels. The supervisory levels directly control the operatives (grassroots level workers). The supervisors link the operatives with other levels of management above them. Each level of management has a distinctive function to perform in the organisation.

Every organisation establishes a number of functions extension is no exception. Some of the common functions are finance, supply, personnel development, manufacture operations, marketing, industrial relations and public relations. The management of an organisation is concerned with:

1. Setting the objectives
2. Formulating plans, policies
3. Procedures and methods for reaching those objectives
4. Organising necessary resources
5. By using standards, rules, directives and feedback, it controls the activities of the organisation, so that the plans and goals are fulfilled.

Functions of a Supervisor (Bruce Yuiel, 1968)

a) Planning
b) Organising
c) Staffing
d) Directing
e) Controlling
f) Coordinating

How Supervision Helps in Organisations (Extension Organisation)

1. It helps in defining work roles to subordinates.
2. It helps in defining a supervisor's role in job relations.
3. It helps in implementing policies and programmes.
4. problem solving

Steps

a) Define the objective.

b) Gather facts and make assumptions.

c) Decide the cause for the problems.

d) Develop several solutions.

e) Select most practical solution.

f) Evaluate the effectiveness of solution adopted.

5. It helps in—teaching the subordinates how to carry out their tasks.
6. It helps in giving orders to subordinates—of written orders, oral orders
7. It helps in job specification for selection—it is a list of qualifications required for the performance of a job. These qualifications are expressed in terms of certain factors such as training, experience, skill, mental ability, dexterity, etc.
8. It helps in giving assistance to subordinates—facilitating work with subordinates by supplying necessary materials.
9. It helps in motivation to subordinates—awards/rewards
10. It helps in building good relationships with superior.
11. It helps in building pressures on supervisors.
12. It helps in assessing individual needs and performance.
13. It helps in counselling subordinates, common in police department and banking sector.

14. It helps in transfer, promotions and demotions.
15. It helps in taking disciplinary action.

Effectiveness of Supervisors in Extension

Madukwe (1993) argues that supervision is not effective due to outside job description activities, as a result extension supervisors are not effective in supervision and it is low to medium.

Summary ratings of supervisory effectiveness

Task area	*Mean score*	*Rating*
Administration	2.67	Medium
Human relation	2. 51	Medium
Coordination	2.50	Medium
Evaluation	2.39	Medium
Training	2.25	Low
Programme planning	2.41	Low

Most of the extension supervisors were spending their time more on office work than other activities.

Duty area	*Mean number of time spent / week*	*Percentage of total time spent*
A. Office work (Excluding that of supervision)	23	57.5
B. Supervision of field extension agents	10	25.0
C. Others: distribution of farm inputs	7	17.0
	40	100.0

Problems of Extension Supervisors Relating to Supervision

	Problems	*Percent*
1.	Work overloaded	95.8
2.	Understaffing	95.8
3.	Disregard of job description	64.8
4.	Interference from supervisors	47.9
5.	Poor training of supervisors	16.9
6.	Mobility problems	5.6

Most of the supervisors rated "over-workload" and understaffing as most important followed by other problems.

Common Extension Management Problems (Adams, 1982)

1. Weak management, complex organisation structure, lack of support to the frontline staff, ill-defined work programme, no incentive to improve.
2. Extension workers are inadequately trained.
3. Extension message ill-adopted to management objectives of small farmers.
4. Lack of support services and support to village staff
5. Understaffing: (India—1:200, Mexico- 1:1000)
6. Diversion of staff from agricultural work.
7. Lack of feedback from field.

Role of Supervision in Extension Administration—A Case

Under Indian conditions the pace of agricultural development to a large extent will be determined by the efforts of extension service put in transferring technology to farmer's fields, and channellise their problems to the subject matter by specialists and scientists for solution and further research.

Any formal organisation has many levels of hierarchy. It may be top policy matters, administrators, technical staff (SMS under T&V system), supervisory staff and grassroots level workers. However, our experience with many extension approaches reveals that we had more levels of supervisory staff than actual field workers (Community Development Project to Watershed Approach). In this context, what the supervisory roles of extension personnel in extension administration are is the main purpose of this paper.

Although training and visit system has got certain virtues of its own, it is mainly criticised for too many levels of hierarchy in developed countries (India). This is one of the most popular extension approaches tried in more than 45 countries in the world. Under this project what the supervisory roles of extension supervisors are and who the extension supervisors in T and V system are form the two issues attempted here.

Before proceeding further, it is worthwhile to know supervisors under T and V system, launched in India. The discussion relating to supervision in T and V is confined to Karnataka State under T and V system.

Organisation pattern

Director of Agriculture	Policy makers
↓	
Addl. Director	
↓	
Joint Directors	
↓	
Deputy Directors	Administrative staff and supervision
↓	
Asst. Directors	
↓	
A.O./SMS	
↓	Technical and supervisory staff
Agril. Extn. Officers	
↓	
Agril. Assts.	Field workers/staff

This organisation pattern is only to help our discussion in the class to make it more lucid.

The materials for discussion includes findings of research studies and are based on literature available on the topic.

Supervisory Roles of Supervisors—Some Empirical Evidences Linking Roles of Extension Supervisors, Subject Matter Specialists and Research Workers

Dudhani (1980) has conducted a study in Karnataka on supervisors (Deputy Directors) Subject matter specialists (Dy. Director (SMS) and Assistant Director of Agriculture, and elicited their major and minor roles in extension administration. The five broad roles are:

1. Conducting trials
2. Preparing schedule of recommendations of improved practices for use of extension workers.
3. Maintaining liaison with research workers.
4. Organising training for in-service personnel.
5. Preparing subject matter for journals.

Linking Role Functions of DDA (SM) under Broad Roles

1. Finding out new information from research stations.
2. Visiting research stations from time to time and knowing practices to be tested.
3. Preparing annual plans for adaptive trials.
4. Transmitting annual plans to districts in time.
5. Visiting districts and discussing plans.
6. Preparing instructional sheets for guidance and conducting trials.
7. Making arrangements for inputs.
8. Random visits to trial plots.

9. Obtaining results for processing data.
10. Sending data for variety release committee.

Organising Training for Inservice Personnel

1. Helping in devising syllabus and curriculum
2. Assistance in developing course outline.
3. Assist DDs in assessing the need of staff.
4. Communicating latest technical information to training programme.
5. Participation in division level training programme.
6. Participation in state level training programme.
7. Helping ADs and training institute in effective use of teaching aids relating to the subject matter.
8. Helping in developing information material, like leaflets, charts, etc.
9. Developing teaching aids suitable for the subject matter.

Veerabhadraiah and Ashok Kumar (1985) revealed the supervisory roles as follows:

Supervisory Roles of Assistant Directors

1. Organising exhibitions for farmers.
2. Organising demonstrations for farmers.
3. Organising training programmes.
4. Organising study tours.

Deputy Directors of Agriculture (Administration)

1. Developing package of practices for farmers and staff.
2. Establishing information centre at the district level.
3. Publishing popular literature.

4. Publishing success stories.
5. Maintaining contact with sister departments.
6. Organising training for officials in the field.

Dy. Directors of Agriculture (Subject matter)

1. Conducting trials.
2. Preparing schedule of recommendations for the use of extension workers.
3. Maintaining liaison with research workers in the state and outside the state.
4. Organising training to inservice personnel.
5. Preparing abstracts from journals and maintaining index cards.

Nataraju (1989) has investigated the supervisory role preferences of Assistant Directors of Agriculture (ADS) under NAEP in Karnataka. He cites the following roles as perceived by ADs:

Essential Roles

1. Spend at least three days each week in the field visiting farmers, AAO and AAs.
2. Make pre-scheduled and surprise visits to ascertain that AAOs, SMS and AAs are fulfilling their duties and to improve the quality of work by offering constructive advice and guidance.
3. Adjust the visit schedules and work procedures of AAs, AAOs and SMS in the light of observations from field visits.
4. Coordinate with other ADAs of cluster in order to utilise the services of AD (SMS) effectively with its entire area of jurisdiction.
5. Ensure that F/N training sessions are held punctually, are well organised and are practically oriented, and all parties

(AAs, AAO SMS representatives of input agencies and any required special trainers) are attended.

6. Ensure that appropriate simple teaching aids and other training materials are available as and when needed.
7. Recommendations and impact points are clearly identified.
8. Ensure that AA, AAO, who is unable to attend is fully briefed on the training content as soon as possible after a session.
9. Meeting AAO and SMS early on the day of F/N training session to review progress in the adoption of recommendations by farmers, field problems, seasonal conditions, availability of inputs, market conditions.
10. Ensuring inclusion of significant points for discussions in the F/N training session.
11. Active participation in F/N training sessions and monthly and seasonal zonal workshops.
12. Through participation in F/N training and monthly workshops, as well as through individual informal efforts, ensure that field problems are brought to the attention of research and solutions reach AAO, AA and farmers.
13. Estimate the demand for inputs based on seasons production programme.
14. Review of estimate demand of inputs in F/N training session with AA, AAO and representative of the input agency.
15. Ensuring demand estimate has reached the appropriate authority.
16. Collecting information on market supply and prices and availability.
17. Informing PAOs on discrepancies in supply and demand.
18. Ensuring actual input availability.
19. Collecting information on pest and disease menace and discussing in F/N training session with PAO.

20. Arranging mobility for field staff.
21. Ascertaining that extension staff are engaged exclusively in extension.

Supporting Duties

22. Taking prompt action under emergencies.
23. Ensuring institutional agencies in training sessions of AAs and AAOs.
24. Being responsible for quality control and inputs control.
25. Discussing with credit agencies and dealers about their requirement and estimates.
26. Assisting SMS in communicating technical problems to agricultural universities for action.
27. Writing confidential reports down below and AO (SMS).
28. Attending to other works assigned by higher ups to the extent possible.

Broad Role and Functions of SMS (Plant Protection) A.O (Katteppa, 1985)

1. Imparting practical training to AAO and AO in his subject.
2. Preparing plant protection recommendations required in the area for each season and training session in consultation with research organisation.
3. Visiting regularly as per planned schedule and surveying the pest/disease incidence.
4. Advising AAs at fortnightly meetings on plant protection problems.
5. Attending monthly workshops at SAUs.
6. Organising field days on plant protection.
7. Preparing literature on plant protection and making available to the Assistant Director.

8. Transmitting complicated and unsolved problems to UAS for solution.
9. Submitting periodical reports to ADA.
10. Guiding AAO and AAs on technical matters.

Broad Role and Functions of SMS (Farm Information and Training)

1. Organising periodical training programmes to AAOs and AAs.
2. Arranging to obtain teaching aids: charts, slides, film, etc.
3. Responsible for production/printing of extension literature and distribution among AAs and farmers.
4. Preparing department reports.
5. Submitting periodical reports.
6. Arranging workshops, seminars, and conducted tour to farmers.
7. Arranging field days and exhibitions.
8. Liaisoning with All India Radio and Press.

Sharma (1968) identified the following roles of AEOs for planning and supervision of agricultural extension programmes at the block level.

1. Setting up agricultural production committees at the village and block level to ensure people's participation.
2. Ensuring agreement of all concerned officials and non-officials on the principles to be kept in view of planning agricultural programmes for the block.
3. Preparing time schedule of different agricultural extension and development activities.
4. Collecting of basic agricultural information at the block level.
6. Assisting block level committees in establishing priorities based on major problems.

7. Allocating resources for progressive execution on the basis of established priorities.
8. Helping Panchayati Samiti to determine the objectives of development programmes.
9. Preparing annual plan of work.
10. Coordinating the efforts of other agencies.

Supervisory Role of Assistant Agricultural Officer (AAO)

1. Guiding and training AAs in their range and involving in technical problems.
2. Working with AAs circle in the field.
3. Visiting AAs circle as per monthly schedule.
4. Ascertaining that farmers are receiving technical recommendations.
5. Checking AA's regular visits.
6. Overseing adoption of technical recommendation by farmers.
7. Ensuring selection of contact farmers as per guidelines.
8. Reviewing the diaries of AAs.
9. Participating in fortnightly training.
10. Ascertaining all AAs participation in fortnightly training.
11. Assisting SMS (AD) to conduct farm trials.
12. Assisting AAs and AOs in conducting field days.
13. Regulating input supply.
14. Maintaining good relations with other departments.

Sharma *et al.* (1987) have investigated the role expectation of Rural Agricultural Extension Officer of T and V System in Madhya Pradesh. He cites the important roles expected from RAEO's:

Sl. No.	Role expectation dimensions	Role performance		
		Always	Seldom	Never
1.	Organising farmers' meeting	70	26	6
2.	Maintaining daily work diary	74	22	4
3.	Visiting of farmers field on fixed time	59	23	18
4.	Knowledge of latest research	47	24	29
5.	Listening to farmers problems	68	20	12
6.	Maintaining notes of new technology	42	36	22
7.	Maintaining demonstration records	53	29	18
8.	Arranging farmers' meetings from time to time	57	16	27
9.	Enabling farmers to get loans	37	24	39
10.	Supplying seeds and other inputs	20	25	55
11.	Maintaining record of research	31	24	45
12.	Arranging farmers' visit to progressive farmers field	49	28	23
13.	Contact with ADOs and SMS	60	21	19
14.	Attending meeting at the head-quarters in time.	172	12	78
15.	Keeping contact with SMS and other depts. to get their cooperation	10	25	66

Dudani (1980) cites group perception indexes of specific roles under broad function conduction trials:

Specific Role Function

1. Finding out new information from the research station
2. Visiting research stations and knowing practices to be tested.
3. Preparing annual plans for adaptive trials.
4. Transmitting annual plans to different districts in time.
5. Discussing plans in different districts.

6. Preparing instructional sheets for guidance for conducting trials.
7. Making arrangements for obtaining inputs in time.
8. Random visit to trial plots in each district.
9. Obtaining results of plots and processing the data.
10. Sending data to variety release committee.

RESEARCH STUDY

1. Procedures of conducting extension programme planning.
2. Identification of the role expectations of extension workers.
3. Measuring extension workers knowledge on various aspects of extension work.
4. Difficulties in planning effective agricultural programmes.
5. Planning and effectiveness of farm production plans.
6. People's involvement in planning extension programmes.

Concern for Future Research

1. Effective methods of training extension workers.
2. Extension/Agricultural policy research need to effective implementation of programmes.
3. Organising for planning.
4. Decision making theories and situation analysis.
5. Programme implementation/action.
6. Evaluation of results (monitoring and evaluation). Sandhu (1994).

Factors Determining Effective Span of Control (Kuntz, 1984)

1. Subordinate training

2. Clarity of delegation of authority
3. Clarity of plans
4. Use of objective standards
5. Communication techniques
6. Amount of personal contact
7. Type of organisation structure
8. Ability of executives
9. Time availability for supervision
10. Nature of work
11. Degree of decentralisation
12. Facilities for staff.

Chelladurai (1997) has investigated the managerial effectiveness of agricultural university/development project in line with broad-based extension system in western, Northwestern and Cauvery delta zones. He comes to an interesting conclusion that majority of the agricultural development officers (59 per cent) were found to be effective in their managerial effectiveness as perceived by their superiors compared to other categories. Table 7.1 gives details of this fact.

Table 7.1

Sl. No.	*Managerial effectiveness category*	*No.of respondents*	*Percent*
1.	More effective	23	23.00
2.	Effective	59	59.00
3.	Less effective	18	18.00

Further, the characteristics like organisational commitment, satisfaction, organisational climate, achievement, motivation, training undergone, experience in service and educational status were associated with managerial effectiveness

Some of the important problems which hamper the managerial effectiveness as opined by Agricultural Development Officers are as under:

Sl No.	*Problem*	*Number*	*Percent*
1.	Low procurement price	81	81
2.	Inadequate advance	81	81
3.	Inadequate staff	80	80
4.	Inadequate physical facilities	78	78
5.	Heavy work load	78	78
6.	Diversified work and ineffective evaluation	77	77
7.	Lack of funds for publicity	74	74
8.	Lack of provision for stationeries	74	74
9.	Dual auditing	75	75
10.	Lack of funds for demonstration and seminars	70	70
11.	Poor storage facility	68	68
12.	Belated communication on budgets and guidelines	65	65
13.	More script work	60	60

Experiences and Thoughts on Supervision

Supervision had its origin in the last quarter of the 19th century. Officers known as 'Special supervisors' appeared, selected usually from the special teachers of the new subjects then entering the curriculum. The problem and procedures growing out of the ever increasing staff of supervisory officials will be treated at length.

Changing Concepts of Supervision

The purpose and philosophy of controlling supervision have gone through a number of significant changes. Supervision at first was largely inspection to determine the state of affairs.

Today, supervision is greatly affected by the increasing insight into the aim of education, the relation of education to the society in which it exists, by the scientific method and by the democratic philosophy. So, supervision is becoming participatory and cooperative, that is, democratic and is increasingly oriented toward the fundamental aims of education and of society. Overlap as well as some antagonism, exist between various schools of thought. A brief summarisation of the older conceptions will therefore be in order before we elaborate on the desirable modern aims and principles.

Supervision under laissez-faire

The teachers in educational institutions were to be inspected, rated, indexed. The technique was inspection unaided by any objective controls. The criticism or rating was as far as the procedure went. If no improvement resulted, or if no detrimental situations developed well, that was not a matter of great concern; if teachers wanted to improve, they were free to do so. If they did not, nothing much was done unless serious trouble resulted; efforts were made not to improve the teacher or the situation but to eliminate the teacher. This ancient theory of supervision persists far more widely than is thought. Lazy and incompetent superintendents and supervisors excuse their inability and failure to give leadership by saying that their teachers are left "free", they are not to be "imposed upon" or "directed". A few call this "democratic" supervision! It is nothing but good old laissez faire!

Supervision as Coercive

This conception was a step away form laissez faire. It was stimulated by recognition of the definite lack of training and the low level of efficiency manifested by many teachers. Teachers needed to be improved. A natural conception of free democratic thinking was that coercion was a means to this end. Responsibility and authority also reside in the upper administrative levels.

Teachers are to carry out directions, and learning is looked upon as a mathematical process which can be directed in definite grooves. The teacher is corrected in her detailed techniques through the handing out of readymade procedures. The teacher is sometimes introduced to the aims to be achieved. Modern democratic supervision goes to the opposite of coercion and regards all educational workers as co-workers in the improvement of education.

The weakness of coercive supervision are:

1. This concept assumes that there are known best methods of doing anything. These are in the possession of the supervisor.
2. This concept is destructive of personality, values particularly, initiative and originality. Inhibitions and even complexes may result.
3. This concept has set up a highly improper relationship between supervisors and teachers. Fear and distrust enter and insincerity and dishonesty result.

Supervision as Training and Guidance

This school of thought is of the favour that guidance comes from above but there was clearly the thought that the training was for improvement to be directed toward the betterment of the teacher himself as well as of his technique. Personal and cultural development was indicated. However, the improvement of personality was recognised as important. But, self-development by extension teachers is not yet seen clearly. But, training and guidance today dominate a great deal of supervisory effort.

Supervision as Democratic Leadership

1. Education is increasingly conceived as a basic social force concerned with the development of human personality and

of a stable democratic social order. Education is not mechanical routine fulfilled through mechanical administration of details. Supervision becomes a fundamental aspect of education, not the thinking enforcement of techniques and causes of study.

2. The necessary techniques of education and of supervision cannot be selected until remote purposes have been clearly understood.
3. Cooperation among agencies which deal with childhood and youth with their protection and education is inescapable. Supervision needs to become coextensive with or at least intimately related to the total setting for learning.

Supervision Increasingly Derived from the Situation Instead of Imposed upon It

The influence of more critical thinking about education in general, of increased use of the scientific method, of greater reliance upon the cooperative attitudes and methods of democracy have combined to bring about a supervision based upon and derived from a given situation rather than imposed upon that situation.

Supervision Affected by the Constant Upgrading of Teacher Training

The focus in recent years is on training teachers in service because teachers were undertrained and leadership to train teachers was overlooked. However, teachers were required to undertake summer courses, but principals and supervisors and administrators were not. The improvement of teachers is not so much a supervisory function in which teachers participate but a teachers function in which supervisors co-operate. Therefore, improvement of the staff in service, coupled with the emphasis upon self-initiated and self-directed programmes of study and development, the improvement function of supervision takes on a wider scope and greater importance.

A MODERN DEFINITION OF SUPERVISION

Modern supervision is for more extensive than of earlier days. The basic principles and attitudes have changed greatly; the trends previously outlined may be summarised:

1. Supervision includes critical thinking about the nature of education and its relation to individual and society.
2. Supervision is increasingly objective and experimental in its methods (stems from scientific movement).
3. Supervision is increasingly participatory and cooperative (policy and plan formulation through group discussion).
4. Supervisory activities and opportunities are distributed among a large number of persons.
5. Supervision is increasingly derived from the given situation rather than imposed upon it.

A MODERN DEFINITION

Supervision deals with those items which primarily and rather directly condition learning and growth. Supervision is leadership and the development of leadership within groups which are cooperative.

a) Evaluating the educational product in the light of accepted objectives of education.
b) Studying teaching-learning situation to determine the antecedents of satisfactory and unsatisfactory growth and achievement of pupils.
c) Improving teaching-learning situations.
d) Evaluating objectives, methods and outcomes of supervision.

Relation Between Administration and Supervision

Administration is generally associated with providing materials, facilities, financing, securing adequate staff, securing books, preparing budget, establishing standards of progress, etc.

Supervision denotes the relationship between employees and their boss or teachers and students who are trained for teaching. Therefore, little discrimination can be made between these two and it is arbitrary. So administration also encompasses supervision (Vashist, 1994:38). However, administrative and supervision duties are overlapping and it is an integral part of administration.

CRITICISMS ON SUPERVISION

Supervision is not free from criticism from the subordinates. Some of the criticisms made in the field of extension education are as follows:

1. Supervision costs too much (finance and policy).
2. Supervision is undemocratic. It destroys the individuality and initiative, and inhibits and interferes with self-reliance and self-expression.
3. Supervision lacks basic principles that are objective, valid and reliable; it lacks adequate criteria for self-evaluation.
4. Supervision lacks staff and adequate training.
5. Supervision lacks a planned programme.

REFERENCES

Adams, 1982, *Agriculture extension in developing countries*, Longman Group Pub. U.K.

Anonymous, 1994, *Annual Report,* Karnataka State Depart-ment of Agriculture, Bangalore.

Anonymous, 1985, *Research in Extension*, Symposium Proceedings, UAS, Bangalore.

Bruce, Yuiel, 1968, *Supervision, principles and techniques,* George Allen Pub. London.

Charles *et al.*, 1983, *Supervision*, The Dryden Press, Mexico.

Chelladurai, 1997, *Managerial effectiveness of agricultural development officers—an assessment.* MSc (Agriculture) Thesis (Unpub.) T.N.A.U, Coimbatore.

Dudani, C.M., and K.A. Jalihal, 1987, Extension, Role Expectations and Role Perception of Subject Matter Specialists, *Ind. J. of Extn. Edn.* 23 (3&4)

Katteppa, Y., 1985, A study on the subject matter specialists in T and V system of Karnataka: role analysis, Ph.D. Thesis (Unpub.), UAS, Bangalore.

Mudukwe, M.C., 1993, Effectiveness of agricultural extension supervisors, *Ind. J. Ext. Edu.* 29 (3 & 4).

Nataraju, A.C., 1989, A study on role performance of ADAs in NAEP in Karnataka, M.Sc. Thesis (Unpub.), UAS, Bangalore.

Rao, M.K. Sethu and C. Bhaskar 1981, Time and task analysis of agricultural development officer, *Mysore J. Agril. Sci.,* 15: 465-467.

Sharma, M.L. *et al.* 1988, Role expectation and role performance of RAEOs *Ind. J. Ext. Edn.*, 24 (3 & 4).

Sandhu, A.S., 1994, *A text book on programme planning,* Oxford Pub. Co., New Delhi.

Vashista, S.R., 1994, *Principles of educational supervision*, Anmol Pub. Pvt. Ltd., New Delhi.

Annexure-I

Organisational Set up of the Directorate of Agriculture

STATE HEAD QUARTERS

Director

Addl. Director (Development)	Administration	Personal Section	Accounts	Addl. Director (Soil Conservation)
	DDA (Headquarters)-1 Adm. Officers (AEP)-2 Admn.Assts.-2		CAO-Cum-Financial Advisor-1 Accounts Officer (SCN)-1 Accounts Asst. -1 Admn. Officer AEP-1	

Addl. Director (Development)

JDA (Devt.)			*JDA (Trg)*	*JDA (Pulses)*		
Development Planning	Statistics DDS (Agri.)	Farm Management	DDA (Danida) AAD(Trg.)	Cereal Crops	Pulses DDA	Oilseeds DDA
DDA (Devel.)		DDA(FM)		DDA	(Pulses & Sunflower)	(Oilseeds)
ADA (Devel.)		ADS (Agri.)		(Crop Botany)		
ADA(Planning)						

JDA (Inputs)			*JDA (Sugarcane)*			*JDA(Quality Control)*	
Plant Protection	Flert& Manures	Seeds	Cotton	S-Cane	Tobacco	Soil Chemistry	Inst.lab.
DDA(PP)	DDA(FCL)	DDA(Seeds)	DDA	DDA	DDA	DDA	DDA
DDA(Ent)	ADA(Manures)	ADA(SI)	(Cotton)	(S-Cane)	(Tobacco)	(Soil Health)	(ICL)
DDA(Pathology)		ADA(STL)					

(Contd...)

(Contd...)

Addl. Director (Development)

JDA (Field Trials)

Farm Information QDA(inf)
AO(inf)
AO(FR)
CAO-Cum-AVS
Photo & Film Officer

Agronomy
DDA
(Agro)

AEP Cell
DDA(AEP)

Engg.
Executive
Engg.
(Civil)

Addl. Director (Soil Conservation)

JDA (Soil Conservation)

Soil Survey
DDA(SS)
ADA(Soil Survery)
AO (Soil Survery)

Soil Conservation
AO(SCN)

JDA (Water Use)

Water Use
DDA(Water Use)

Divisional Level

1

Divisional J.D.A.

1

Staff of the Dn. Headqtrs.

DDA(H.Q.)
Adm. Officer
Adm. Asst.
Agri. Officer (Farm Information)

Other Staff at District & Taluk Level in each division

1	2	3	4
Bangalore Dn Bangalore Rural Bangalore Urban Tumkur & Kolar Dists. 1) PAOS (DDAS)-4 2) DDA (FT & EC) Chillanahally 3) DDA (SCN?) Tumkur & Kolar	Shimoga Dn (Shimoga & Chitradurga Districts) 1) PAOS (DDAS)-2 2) DDA (FT & EC)-Hiriyur " Bhadravathi " Thyavaagi 3) " (SCN) Shimoga & Chitradurga	Mysore Dn. (Mysore, Mandya, Kodagu) 1) PAOS (DDAS)-3 2) DDA (RDTC)-Mandya Kuidge 4) DDA (IJAEIC)-Mandya 5) ADA(ADC)-Sathanur 6) DDA(SCN)-Mysore	Hasan Dn. (Hassan, D. Kannada Chickmagalur Dists.) 1) PAOS(DDAS)-3 2) DDA(SCN)-Hassan

Staff of the Dn. Headqtrs.		Other Staff at District & Taluk Level in each division	
DDA (H.Q.) *Adm. Officer* *Adm. Asst.* *Agri. Officer (Farm Information)*			
5	6	7	8
Belgaum Dn.	Dharwad Dn.	Raichur Dn.	Gulbarga Dn.
(Belgaum & Bijapur Dist.)	(Dharwad & UK Dists.)	(Raichur & Bellary Dists)	(Gulburga & Bidar Dists)
1) PAOS (DDAS)-2	1) PAOS (DDAS)-2	1) PAOS (DDAS)-2	1) PAOS (DDAS) -2
2) DDA (FT&EC)-Jamkhandi	2) DDA (RDTC)-Dharwad	2) DDA (FT&EC) Gangavathi	2) DDA (SCN) Gulbarga
" Arabhavi	3) ADA (ADC)-Dharwad	3) ADA (ADC)-Dhadesugur	
3) DDA (RDTC) -Bagalkot	"" Konnur	4) DDA (SCN)-Raichur & Bellary	
4) ADA (ADC) Jambagi	4) " (STL) Dharwad		
"Jamkhandi	5) DDA (SCN)-Dharwad		
5) DDA (SCN)-Belgaum & Bijapur			

DISTRICT LEVEL
Principal Agricultural Officer (DDA)

ADA(Hqr)	ADA(Inputs)	SMS Team (3)	Adm. Asst.	A.O.(F.M.)
		1) ADA & Trg.)	(For Admn. & Accounts)	
		2) ADA (P.P.)		
		Taluk A.D.A.		

AEOS	SMS Team at
AAS	Central Taluk
	1. AO (Crop Production)
	2. AO (Plant Protection)
	3. AO (Information)

Note: 1. At the Dist. Level PAO (DDA) is in overall charge of Development work. There are 175 taluks in the State out of which 60 are Central taluks. Each taluk will have an Asst. Director of Agriculture. He will guide and superwise the work of extension staff in his taluk under AEP.

2. Each Central taluk covers a cluster of 2 to 4 taluks. Each central taluk has a team of SMS consisting of 3 specialists. They work under the control of the central taluk ADA who is also designated as ADA (Co-ordination). ADA (Co-ordination) will ensure that the SMS team stationed in his taluk serve all the taluks in the cluster according to fixed schedule.

3. There are 750 AAO designated as AEOs working under AEP. The AEO would supervise and guide the work of 6 to 8 Agricultural Assts.

4. There are 5200 Agri. Assts. working under AEP in the State. One A.A. is provided for about 400-800 farm families.

Expansion of Abbreviation used: JDA-Joint Director of Agriculture, CAO-Chief Accounts Officer, DDA-Deputy Director of Agriculture, DDS-Deputy Director of Statistics, PAO-Principal Agricultural Officer. ADA-Asst. Director of Agriculture, FT&EC-Farmers Training & Education Centre, SCN/SC-Soil Conservation, RDTC-Rural Development Training Centre, ADC-Agricultural Development Centre, IJAETC-Indo Japanese Agriculture & Extn. Training Centre, FM-Farm Management, SI-Seed Inspector, STL-Seed Testing Laboratory, QC-Quality Control, FCL-Fertilizer Control Laboratory, FR-Farm Radio, ICL-Insecticide Control Lab, AO- Agricultural Extn. Officer, SMS-Subject Matter Specialist, PP-Plant Protection, AAS-Agricultural Assistants.

STAFF IN POSITION OF THE DIRECTORATE OF AGRICULTURE, BANGALORE

Sl. No.	Category of Post	*No. Sanctioned*			*Staff in Position*			*Vacant*		
		Crop Husbandry	*Soil Conservation*	*Total*	*Crop Husbandry*	*Soil Conservation*	*Total*	*Crop Husbandry*	*Soil Conservation*	*Total*
1.	Director of Agriculture	1	—	1	1	—	1	—	—	—
2.	Add. Director of Agri.	2	1	3	2	1	3	—	—	—
3.	Joint Director of Agri.	16	1	17	13	1	14	3	—	3
4.	Dv. Director of Agri.	75	20	95	63	19	82	12	1	13
5.	Asst. Director of Agri.	346	5	351	291	5	296	55	—	55
6.	Agricultural Officers	363	63	426	259	59	318	104	4	108
7.	Asst. Agri. Officers	1470	500	1970	1350	496	1846	120	4	124
8.	Agri. Assts.	5200	2670	7870	3044	2109	5153	2156	561	2717
	Total	7473	3260	10733	5023	2690	7713	2450	570	3020
	Others	3809	1571	5380	3614	1554	5168	195	17	212
9.	Grand Total	11282	4831	16113	8637	4244	12881	2645	587	3232

Source: Directorate of Economics & Statistics.

Annexure-II

The Art of Delegation

—Dr R.D. Agarwal

Managers do recognise the need of effective delegation as a tool of time management, development and motivation of employees, enhancement of the quality and speed of decisions, etc. However, most of them lack adequate skills in the art of delegation. They are faced with the problems of deciding what, how, when, how much and to whom to delegate responsibilities and authority. This paper provides certain guidelines to managers in making these decisions.

Delegations is situational. The delegating manager has to consider the criticality of the decision, abilities and competence of his subordinates, the operating situation, etc., while making his delegation decisions. He also has to set up an adequate control system in order to ensure that targets and goals are achieved, and authority is used discretely and judiciously. He has to make modifications in his delegation in response to changes in his internal and external environment. Delegation is thus a dynamic process, and the manager needs to keep his delegation fine-tuned to operating situations. It should be adequate in order to be effective, and adequate is a matter of dynamic equilibrium.

Most managers recognise the need for delegation but are unable to delegate due to lack of skills in the art of delegation. In a workshop on delegation conducted by the author, several managers expressed difficulties in deciding what to delegate, when to delegate, how much to delegate, whom to delegate, how to delegate, etc. Their typical comments are listed here:

a) I want to delegate but who to delegate? I have nobody whom I can trust.

b) How can I delegate when I am responsible for results ?

c) I don't delegate because I know I can make the right decisions at the right time.

d) If I delegate to others who will listen to me ?

e) If I delegate, won't subordinates gain power over me and in my department?

f) It is faster if I do it myself.

g) I am willing to delegate but my boss asks me so many questions that I have to keep track of everything that happens around here.

This paper focuses on these areas of delegation with a view to helping managers in delegating effectively.

WHAT IS DELEGATION?

Delegation is the process of:

a) assignment of tasks, activities and responsibilities and subordinates.

b) transfer of authority so as to enable them to makes necessary decisions, utilise resources and command others for performing the assigned tasks and activities, and to discharge responsibilities.

c) extraction of accountability for adequate performance and for producing the desired results.

d) setting up an adequate monitoring and control system so as to keep track of progress on assigned tasks, activities and responsibilities, measure performance and take corrective action.

WHY DELEGATE?

Delegation is the means by which a manager can enhance his capabilities by capitalising on those of his subordinates: Since a manager has only a limited time at his disposal, he can utilise it most effectively by entrusting less important tasks to his responsibilities. Delegation is also a powerful tool of training, developing and motivating the subordinates.

Effective Time Management

A manager can manage his time most effectively by delegating adequately. It frees him from the important aspects of his job so that he can devote his time to those aspects where failure or lack of performance will seriously endanger results.

For example, the more a production manager involves himself in handling day-to-day production problems, management of the shop floor, etc., the less time does he gets for determination of production goals, planning, organising and controlling pro-duction, for coordination with purchasing, marketing and quality control, and for keeping himself abreast with new development in technology, methods and processes, etc.

The more he can delegate the routine, day-to-day affairs to his subordinates, the more time he can gain to do things which are major areas of his responsibilities, which demand his attention, which he alone can do and which nobody else can do. The more time he devotes to do the 'urgent' things, like machine break-down, shortage of labour complement, of a case of indiscipline on the shop floor, the less time does he get to do the 'important' things involving planning, coordination and control. Urgent things demand attention here and now but do not have long-term impact on performance.

Important things like goal-setting, long-range planning, etc., can be postponed for tomorrow but they are critical to a manager's performance and have long-term impact on his success. The time for important things can be created by delegating more and more urgent things to the subordinates.

Enhancement of Capabilities by Capitalising on Those of Others

A manager can multiply his own capacities by assigning duties and responsibilities to his subordinates. He can maximise his own managerial inputs to task performance by optimising his delegation. When a manager delegates responsibility and authority to his subordinates, he provides them an opportunity to enhance their contribution to the achievement of his own as well as his segmental goals. Delegation thus permits him to enhance his own contribution added with his subordinates' contribution to goal achievement. Many subordinates have abilities far in excess of the requirements of their jobs, and look for opportunities to 'get their teeth into something real hard and challenging', 'to show what they can do given the chance', 'to prove themselves'. These are the people a manager can really capitalise upon to increase theirs as well as his own contribution to goals.

Tool of Training and Developing Subordinates

It is one of the major responsibilities of a manager to provide training to his subordinates and create an environment for their development so as to enable them to perform effectively. Opportunities for growth and development are highly motivating to an employee. They enable him to utilise his highest potential. They provide him challenging opportunities, for his growth and development. It is through delegation of challenging tasks and responsibilities that subordinates learn to take the initiative and responsibility.

Tool of Motivation

Delegation is a powerful tool of motivating the employees. It has been an establishment that it is intrinsic rewards like challenge, responsibility, opportunities for development of abilities, etc., which have much greater motivating effect on them than financial rewards. Delegation is a means of providing these psychological rewards to them. A manager can use it as a means of assigning challenging tasks and responsibilities to his subordinates, encouraging them to take responsibility and initiative, and creating opportunities to use and develop their abilities.

Demonstrates Trust and Confidence

When a manager delegates a task to a subordinate, he is in effect telling him, 'I trust you and. I have confidence in your competence and abilities; I know you will do your best to achieve the desired results'. And when we trust others in this way, they tend to respond to it. This trust and confidence in them is highly motivating to them.

Builds Self-confidence

Delegation helps employees build their self-confidence. As we do we gain self-confidence. As managers perform delegated tasks so they gain self-confidence in their abilities and competence. This self-confidence in their abilities spurs them to try out new tasks, solve difficult problems and face challenging situations. A person, self-confident in his abilities, performs much better than another who is unsure and shaky about himself.

Provides Fresh Ideas and Viewpoints

When a manager delegates tasks and responsibilities to his subordinates, they bring to performance not only renewed energy, but also ideas and viewpoints different from his own.

The manager who appreciates ideas and viewpoints different from his own encourages his delegates to innovate more effective ways of task performance and problem solving. This is what energises the organisation and enables it to face continually changing and challenging environment.

Improves Quality of Decisions

Delegation vests authority in those who are responsible for task performance. It gives decision-making authority to those who have to tackle job-related problems. For example, the foreman is the best person to fully understand the shop situation and production problems. If he also has the authority to solve these problems, the quality of decisions is likely to be better than if these problem-solving decisions were made by someone removed a level or two above in the hierarchy. True, many decisions such as disciplining an employee, choice of technology, layout of the shop, etc., cannot be delegated to first-line supervisors, but if their viewpoints are incorporated in the decisions of higher level managers, the quality of decisions tends to be better. Even if an employee is not fully delegated decision-making authority, but given an opportunity to give his suggestions and ideas, and if his viewpoints are incorporated in decisions, it still amounts to delegation, though partial delegation. A supervisor may not have the authority to discipline or reward an employee, but if his recommendations are given due importance by the decision maker, decisions are likely to be more realistic. Moreover, it permits the supervisor to gain upward influence which strengthens his position in relation to his employee group.

WHAT TO DELEGATE

The most important delegation task the manager faces is to decide what responsibilities, functions, tasks and activities he should delegate to his subordinates or the subordinate group. He begins by analysing his objectives and responsibilities, decisions that have to be made for the accomplishment of these objectives and fulfilment or responsibilities. This analysis will provide him significant insights into what he should not delegate. He may use certain guidelines to help him decide upon his delegation:

1. Criticality of decisions
2. Futurity of decisions
3. Areas of excellence
4. Value involving decisions
5. Relatedness of decisions
6. Recurrent decisions
7. Special assignments
8. Areas of personal responsibility

1. Criticality of Decisions

The manager has to consider criticality of decisions to the fulfilment of his objectives. If the function or responsibility involves decisions which are likely to have a severe impact upon his future success, he may not delegate at all, or only partially delegates such decisions. Even if he partially delegates such decisions, he should deeply involve himself in the decision making process. Distribution channel decision is one such decision for marketing manager. This decision is unstructured, needs a lot of judgement and ingenuity, and it is critical to the achievement of his marketing goals. He may delegate this responsibility if he has reliable and competent subordinates but he should involve himself heavily in the decision making process to ensure that the optimum decision is made. He may delegate the implementation of this decision more fully to his subordinates.

2. Futurity of Decision

Some decisions have a long-term impact on the manager's success. Product decisions fall in this category. Product is a major element in the marketing strategy of an organisation, and product selection, including the generic product, quality, features, shape, size, colour, etc., has a long-term impact on its future survival and profitability. Such decisions cannot be fully delegated. Development of alternative products and analysis of their impact on the future of the organisation may be delegated to the lower level managers, but the final decision must be made by the chief executive.

3. Areas of Excellence

The manager should identify areas where excellence is required for his overall effectiveness. A marketing manager may determine that customer service is the key element of his competition strategy, and excellence in this area would significantly affect his ability to attain his marketing goals. Policy decisions and key administrative decisions in this area may better be made by the marketing managers himself with or without sharing them with his subordinates. Tactical decisions may, of course, be delegated to lower level managers.

4. Value Involving Decisions

Every organisation has certain basic values which it upholds dearly. "Fairness to all in all our dealings" may be one of the values of an organisation. The manager, of course, delegates a myriad of decisions to his lower level managers, and decisions made by him are implemented by many others. Major decisions involving this basic value of "fairness" may well be made by the manager himself. This value should also be incorporated in all decisions made and implemented by his subordinates. The manager should emphasize to his subordinates that they should uphold this value while making and implementing all decisions.

5. Relatedness of Decisions

Some decisions are of a nature which cut across departmental lines. Product decision is one such decision. It has significant production, marketing and financial implications, besides research and development, industrial design, industrial engineering and quality control overtones. Such decisions must be made by the heads of the concerned departments. Decisions which are of a 'local' nature, such as production scheduling, can be easily delegated to the concerned manager.

6. Recurrent Decisions

Some decisions are of a recurrent nature, such as production scheduling decisions, machine allocation decision, etc. In fact, most decisions in any organisation are of a recurrent nature. Policies, systems and procedures are generally available for making such decisions. Furthermore, these decisions are generally of a local nature, are not critical for the overall organisational success and do not have long-term impact on its future survival and profitability. All such decisions should be delegated to appropriate managers. These decisions are not necessarily routine decisions to be made mechanically. In fact, they may involve a lot of initiative, responsibility, imnovativeness and creativity on the part of delegates.

7. Special Assignments

Managers often have special assignments such as identification of areas of cost reduction, investigation into sales decline, gathering and analysing data about compensation by competing units in local community, preparation of sales forecasts, etc. These and other similar special tasks of an occasional nature are appropriate candidates for delegation. These tasks may be delegated not only to experienced, competent and reliable subordinates but also to new and less experienced ones as a means of developing their abilities and interest, and of providing them exposure to various aspects of departmental activities.

8. Areas of Personal Responsibility

The manager should not delegate areas where his personal attention is needed and for which he alone should assume prime responsibility. Some of these areas are maintenance of motivation and morale in the work organisation, administration of reward and punishment, appraisal of performance, interpersonal and interdepartmental relation-ship with peer group or higher echelons of management, sensitive areas of relationships with outside agencies such as bankers, suppliers, customers, etc., resolution of interpersonal and intergroup conflict etc. In these and other similar areas, the manager can often not delegate without jeopardising his own position or exposing the subordinate to unenvious situations.

WHO TO DELEGATE

While deciding upon the areas of delegation, the manager keeps in mind the abilities, skills and personality qualities of his subordinate managers and non-managers to whom he can delegate effectively. He is also cognizant of the need to develop his employees through delegation. He closely relates the needs of delegated tasks, functions and responsibilities with the experience, abilities, motivation, commitment, initiative, sense of responsibility, frustration and ambiguity tolerance, interpersonal skills, etc., of individual members of his subordinate group. The manager may use the following guidelines in deciding whom to delegate responsibility and authority:

1. Delegating to experienced employees
2. Delegating to new employees
3. Maintaining the chain of command
4. Delegation to groups

Subordinates with Experience, Abilities and Personality Qualities

The manager should delegate tasks to subordinates who:

a) have or can be provided with necessary information needed for job performance.
b) have the required level of abilities and competence, or can be trained within the time constraints.
c) are capable of taking initiative and responsibility.
d) possess the requisite interpersonal skills and abilities to work with groups,
e) can work through ambiguous situations and tolerate frustrating experiences.
f) can bring ingenuity, innovativeness and creativity to problem solving.
g) have vision and imagination.
h) are cognizant of the requirements of job performance of the department and the organisation.

It will be rare that the manager would have subordinates with all these and other qualities needed for performing delegated tasks. He has to find the best subordinate available. In case a subordinate lacks in one or more of the aspects which are critical for successful task performance, the manager may resort to partial delegation, and at the same time help the subordinate develop the desired abilities and personality qualities.

New Employees

The manager should delegate to new employees also as he

delegates to experienced ones. However, in the former case, delegation will have to be a partial and step-by-step process. As the new employee gains experience, abilities, competence and confidence, he should be entrusted with more and more delegation. In such cases, delegation is used not only as a means of task accomplishment but also as a tool of training and development.

Chain of Commond

The delegating manager should not violate the chain of command while deciding his delegation. He should delegate only to his immediate subordinate group. In case he deems it essential to delegate to subordinates of his immediate subordinate, he should do so through the latter.

Delegating to the Group

Managers with participative style of leadership, who aim at using as a tool of welding their subordinates into cohesive work-teams, should delegate tasks and responsibilities to groups of subordinates, as far as possible. They may delegate a whole task to a group and let the group decide upon the individual assignments. In this case, the group leader is held accountable for successful task performance.

WHEN TO DELEGATE

Assuming that the manager has already delegated effectively all tasks, activities and functions, he should review his delegation, and make a fresh delegation under the following situations:

1. a new subordinate has been hired or transferred to his unit.

2. an existing subordinate has been promoted.
3. an existing subordinate has demonstrated development of abilities, competence, commitment, etc., or shown eagerness to take additional responsibilities.
4. an existing subordinate is not coming up to expectations.
5. tasks or requirements of task performance have undergone significant changes.
6. new tasks have come up such as an investigation into causes of substandard quality, organising a dealers' convention, etc.
7. a crisis situation has developed such as a rush order, machine breakdown, employees' strike, etc.
8. significant changes have occurred in the environment of business such as emergence of a new competitor, development of a new technology, a new government policy, etc.
9. the manager is himself planning to go on vacations.
10. the manager finds himself under severe time pressure.

HOW MUCH TO DELEGATE

A delegation may be full or partial. In a full delegation, the manager permits the subordinates or the subordinate group full authority to make task-related decisions and implement the same within the framework of organisational policies, procedures and values, and other parameters specified by him. In partial delegation, he delegates only partial authority to do the needful for the accomplishment of the assigned task.

FULL DELEGATION

The manager may delegate certain tasks, functions and responsibilities to his subordinates, and make them fully accountable for the accomplishment of results. A production manager may fully delegate the task of production scheduling, machine loading, manpower allocation, etc., to his subordinate managers within the constraints of production plans and targets. A marketing manager may authorise his field sales supervisors to vary the sales price of a product within the range of five per cent, or to give additional discount up to two per cent over and above the limit of 10 per cent. In such cases, the delegatee makes the decisions within specified parameters and situational constraints. He may, however, be required by the delegating manager to report to him all such cases in his monthly sales reports.

PARTIAL DELEGATION

Delegation is only partial when the delegatee is authorised to make only some of the decisions related to the assigned task, or when he is asked to obtain prior approval of the decision from the delegating manager. Partial delegation may indeed be of various types and shades.

A. Prior Approval

The manager may delegate a task to a subordinate and ask him to make the task-related decisions subject to his prior approval. A production manager may assign to his subordinate the task of preparing the production programme for the next quarter, and obtain his approval before implementation, or a marketing manager may ask his subordinate to negotiate with an advertising agency for launching an advertising campaign, but obtain his approval before finalising his terms and conditions.

B. Set Parameters

The manager may choose to set parameters decision making by his subordinate or subordinate group. A chief executive may ask his administration manager to fix a dinner for the visiting foreign collaborators, and instruct him that they should look for a five-star hotel which specialises in Chinese food, and serves Japanese liquor. In this case, the administration manager has been delegated authority to select any hotel within the parameters stated above.

C. A *Posteriori* Approval

The manager may authorise his subordinate to make his job-related decisions but obtain his approval afterwards to satisfy the rules and regulations. A purchasing manager may ask his subordinate to purchase twenty-five office tables of the specified size and design at the best price and of a reasonably good quality, and afterwards obtain his approval on the purchase order.

D. Decide and Inform

The manager may authorise his subordinate to make his job-related decisions as he thinks fit but inform him about it so that he knows what is going on. A general manager may authorise his public relations manager to spend a certain sum of money for providing scholarships to deserving children of employees, and later on provide him a complete list of children who have been so assisted.

E. Gather and Analyse Information

The manager may ask a subordinate or a group of his subordinates to gather information on a specific aspect of the company, analyse it and present a report.

F. Develop and Evaluate Alternatives

The manager may ask a subordinate or a subordinate group to develop alternatives to solve a specific problem, evaluate the same and recommend the optimum solution to the problem. A production manager may ask one of his subordinates or a subordinate group to develop proposals for cost reduction to the extent of five per cent, evaluate each proposal and make final recommendation as to the best proposal to accomplish the desired results. In this case, the production manager himself finalises the proposal for implementation. He may, however, discuss the proposal with the subordinate or subordinate group before making the final decision. This kind of delegation serves as an excellent tool of training and developing the delegatee or delegatees. It also provides them a sense of worth, the feeling of belongingness, and an opportunity to use their abilities, creativity and innovativeness.

G. Consult the Subordinate or Subordinate Group

The manager may discuss the problem with his subordinate or subordinate group, obtain their ideas, and then make the decision himself. Or, he may present the problem to his subordinate or subordinate group together with his tentative solution, and then seek their reactions and ideas. In this case also, the manager himself makes the decision. A production manager may tell his subordinate or subordinate group that the percentage of quality rejects is above acceptable limits, and ask them to give suggestions for improving the quality. Or, he may present the quality problem to a subordinate or subordinate group, before that the way to improve quality is close supervision, and then ask them what they think about it. The production manager may or may not accept their suggestions while making his final decision for improving quality.

H. Let the Group Decide

The manager may present the problem to the subordinate group and let the group decide upon the problem with himself acting as the group leader. In the above case of quality problem, the production manager may state the problem to the subordinate group, and let the ground decide about the ways and means for improving quality. In this case, the production manager acts as the group leader, and his role is limited to clarifying ideas, channellising discussion, giving his ideas where necessary as any other group member would, and either taking vote or obtaining consensus. Finally, he summarises the decision and spells it out. The decision may or may not be recorded.

How much the manager will delegate to his subordinate or subordinate group will depend on his perception of the task, the subordinate and the situation. He will be inclined to delegate more fully to the extent the tasks are of a recurrent nature, are well structured and are not critical to his own success. Again, he will be inclined to delegate to the extent he has available to himself subordinates who are capable or performing the task, and possess the desired level of integrity, initiative, commitment and responsibility.

HOW TO DELEGATE

The manner in which tasks are delegated is critical to effective delegation. If the manager clearly and unambiguously specifies the delegated task, the expected level of performance and its timeframe provides resources and support during the process of task performance by the delegatee, and sets up an appropriate control system, the delegation is likely to be successful. The following guidelines, based on experience and empirical research, have been developed to help managers delegate effectively:

1. Determine the delegated task.
2. Identify the right person.
3. Specify the scope of authority.
4. Provide policies and procedures.

5. Specify the expected level or performance in terms of results.
6. Involve the delegatee in all delegation decisions.
7. Set up the control system.
8. Provide resources.
9. Inform all concerned about delegation.
10. Provide feedback.
11. Tolerate mistakes.
12. Interference must be minimum.
13. Encourage two-way free communication.
14. Be perceived as a source of help.
15. Avoid upward delegation.

1. Determine the Delegated Task

As a first step to 'how of delegation', the manager must determine in his mind what he wants to delegate and to whom. The personnel manager of a company may decide to delegate the responsibility of managing the canteen to one of his subordinates. First of all, he must decide about the mission of the canteen. Suppose he decides it as 'serve nutritious food to employees at no-profit-no-loss basis'. Following this, he must determine the objectives of the canteen for the current year and for the next five years. The activities and tasks involved will have to be identified. This analysis will provide him a good insight into the tasks, functions and responsibilities involved in the management of the canteen and help him decide upon his delegation.

2. Identify the Right Person

Following the delegation decision, the manager has to identify the 'right' person who has the requisite experience, capabilities, initiative, commitment and human relations skills to perform the delegated task. The personnel manager, in our example, will have to look for a person who has knowledge and experience about food and catering, purchasing and inventory control, leadership quality, interpersonal skills and human relations skills, etc.

3. Specify the Scope of Authority

The manager should, in consultation with the delegatee, determine the authority that the delegatee would need to perform the delegated task. In the canteen example, the canteen manager's authority relating to manpower hiring, firing, disciplining, rewarding, etc., will have to be specified, his financial and purchasing authority will have to be determined, and authority relating to matters such as deciding the menu, pricing the various items, hours of canteen credit sales, etc., will have to be laid down. In some of these matters, the canteen manager may be given full authority, while in others, partial authority. A committee consisting of the personnel manager, production manager, canteen manager and union representative may be set up to make decisions about the menu and the hours of the canteen. It is neither necessary nor possible to lay down the extent of authority of the delegatee in all matters relating to his job performance. The level of initiative he takes, the extent of authority he uses, the amount of leadership he displays, are all matters of superior-subordinate relationships and mutual understanding. A manager takes orders from the situation, and considering his relationship with his superior, decides how far he can go on his own, in what matters he should obtain the decision from his superior, in what matters he should report to him, and so on and so forth. This understanding between them is developed through their day-to-day interactions.

Provide Policies and Procedures

A delegatee should have available to him for his guidance

policies and procedures for decision making and work performance. These policies and procedures should be made, reviewed and revised as and when necessary.

5. Specify the Expected Level of Performance in Terms of Results

The manager must make clear to the delegates the level of performance and the results expected of him. The chief executive of a company may specify to his production manager results in terms of production quantity, quality, cost, employee morale, union relations, quality of life at mark, operative training, machine maintenance, etc. Unless the delegates knows and fully understands his superior's expectations in terms of results, he is without any guidepost, and cannot be expected to produce the desired results.

6. Involve the Delegatee in Delegation Decisions

The manager should discuss delegation with the delegatee so as to gain a common understanding of task and responsibilities, of delegated authority, pertinent policies and procedures, and expected results. This will provide the delegatee an opportunity to point out the difficulties or the hurdles he anticipates, and the resources and guidance he would need for performing the delegated task. Involvement of the subordinate will be highly motivating to him, and gain his commitment to the delegated task and responsibility.

7. Set up the Control System

While the delegating manager delegates task, authority and primary responsibility to the delegatee, his final responsibility to his own superior for delegated tasks remains undiminished. He should, therefore, set up an adequate system to monitor the delegatee's performance. In setting up the control system also, the manager should consult his delegate's subordinate. This will not only help the latter to gain a clear understanding of the kind of reports—oral or written—and the type of reports he is expected to make to his superior. The manager should, however, bear in mind that more control does not necessarily mean effective control. In fact, more control not only is annoying, frustrating and de-motivating to the delegatee, it also results in less effective control. Control should be set at strategic points. Depending on the nature of the delegated task, the delegatee and the situation, the manager may decide to control by results only, or he may consider it necessary to monitor not only the progress of task performance but also decisions, methods and activities critical for task performance and goal achievement. It should be recognised by the manager that delegation and control have an inverse relationship. The greater the control, the lesser is the delegation.

8. Provide Resources

Then manager should, in consultation with the delegatee, decide upon the human, financial and material resources that would be needed by the latter from time to time for task completion. He should ensure that resources are made available to the delegatee as and when needed by him.

9. Inform all Concerned about Delegation

The manager should inform all the concerned in his department and other departments that delegation has taken place so that the delegatee may be able to get their acceptance and cooperation for job performance. These concerned people within and outside his department are all those to whom he has either to provide inputs or obtain outputs, or interact during the course of his job performance.

10. Provide Feedback

As the delegatee progresses in his task, the manager should provide him feedback on his performance. The aim of feedback is to help the delegatee to learn how he is doing. In case of unacceptable performance, the manager must, of course, bring it to his notice, but the purpose of criticism should be not to condemn the delegatee or belittle his achievement and contribution, but to improve his future performance. Criticism should, therefore, be constructive and accompanied with positive suggestions for improvement. Moreover, criticism should be specific, and pinpoint the areas of deficiency rather than of a generalised nature.

In no case should criticism be such as would undermine the self-confidence of the delegatee, or compromise his position, status or organisational standing.

11. Tolerance of Mistakes

We all make mistakes, who doesn't? The only difference between the wise and the stupid is that the former learns from his mistakes whereas the later persists in it. The only way not to make a mistake is not to do anything. Anyone who takes the initiative, is creative and innovative, is bound to maken mistakes. These mistakes must be debited to the cost of learning. The manager should, therefore, be tolerant of the mistakes to his delegatees unless he wants to destroy their initiative and creativity. The only condition is that the mistake must be genuine and bona fide, and the delegatee should learn from his mistake.

12. Interference must be Minimum

Many a manager cannot but breathe down the neck of the delegatee. Others cannot but keep poking their nose in his work. Such managers not only waste their own time and make a nuisance of themselves, but also demotivate the delegatee, make him lose initiative, and demoralise him. He keeps running to the manager for all decisions, just because he finds it less troublesome to do so rather than be bothered by his superior all the time, and answer his unending questions. Therefore, once the manager delegates, he should 'let it go'.

13. Encourage Free Two-way Communication

The manager should encourage two-way communication. The delegatee should feel free not only to discuss his problems and volunteer his ideas and suggestions, but also to let out his frustrations. Such communication can grow only in a non-threatening environment of mutual trust and confidence.

14. Be Perceived as a Source of Help

An effective delegator emphasised colleague relationships rather than superior-subordinate relationships. Like the position of the prime minister in a parliamentary democracy in relation to his cabinet, ministers, the manager is first among equals in his relationship with his subordinates. He is the leader and the facilitator. He is there to inspire and enthuse his delegatees. He is there to help them achieve their goals. He just stands by to be available to help his junior colleagues in case they need his help.

15. Avoid Upward Delegation

The manager should not permit his delegatee to redelegate the task and responsibility back to him. All bucks should not stop at his table, but at appropriate tables. Many managers get confused in ambiguous situations, just cannot make decisions, have a dependent personality and feel uncomfortable when given charge of a situation. They find it easier to obtain decisions from their superiors rather than make their own decisions. But the delegating manager should not permit them to do so. He should insist that they should solve their own problems, that he mould be available for help and guidance as and when needed but he would not let them escape responsibility. If a delegatee comes to him for a decision in a problem situation, he should ask him to work out his own solution, or at least develop alternative solutions for discussion. But if he says, 'Well, I will let you know what to do', the monkey is on his back. The delegatee is free from the burden of having to make the decision after shifting it on to his manager.This should be scrupulously avoided. Don't do their job for them, only help them do their job. That's the way to help people learn and grow.

In sum, delegation is an art. It must be constantly and assiduously developed and refined. Effective delegation is crucial to management effectiveness, to the growth and development of employees, to their morale and self-confidence and to quicken an optimum decision making at all levels. The acid test of effective delegation is that each manager contributes to the best of his abilities and competence, and when the manager is away on a long vacation, or kicked upward, there is always a second-in-command to run the show, and the organisation keeps going as smoothly as in the past.

Annexure-III

Model Question Paper

DAE & RS, CARDS, TNAU, COIMBATORE-3.
AEX 831, SUPERVISION IN EXTENSION ORGANISATION (1 + 1)

MID-SEMESTER THEORY EXAM

Duration : 3 hours
Marks : 30

Answer all major questions and all questions carry equal marks:

1. Giver the meaning and definition of supervision in the context of development administration by comparing yours with that of other authors.
2. Explain the various principles and styles of supervision. How would you apply these in the special situation of rural and agricultural development sector in your state.
3. Compare and contrast following: Answer any four:
   i) Administration Vs Supervision
   ii) Traditional Vs Modern Supervision
   iii) Autocratic Vs Free rein techniques of supervision
   iv) Two factor Vs Life Cycle theory of supervisor.
   v) Manager Vs Supervisor

4. Write an essay on the personal characteristics and qualities of a good supervisor. Explain any one case study/ study based on your exposure or literature.

5. Critically analyse supervisor—subordinate relationship and interaction process. Also explain supervision in development programmes in India. Offer your strategies for effective strengthening their relationship.

FINAL THEORY EXAM

Cite suitable literature and examples.
All Major Questions carry equal marks.

Duration 3 hours
5 x 8 = 40

I. What do you understand by the following concepts relating to Supervision in Extension Organisation?

   1. Qualities and roles of good supervisors.
   2. Case studies on roles of Extension Management.
   3. Improving the supervisor-subordinates relationship.
   4. Techniques of decision making.
   5. Communication as organisational heart-beat.

II. Explain with suitable field situation as to how would you apply the following supervisory aspects in your extension management. Answer any FOUR.

   1. Supervisory management.
   2. Factors determining effective span of control.
   3. Supervision in development programmes.
   4. Steps in extension decision-making.
   5. Organisational communication.

III. Compare and contrast the following supervisory theories/ ideas in the context of extension organisational management, Answer any FOUR.

1. Traditional Vs modern definition of supervision.
2. Synectic technique Vs Delphi technique.
3. Mertis and demerits of group decision making.
4. Coordination Vs cooperation in management.
5. Expectancy Theory Vs contingency Theory of supervisor.

IV. Prepare a comprehensive project or offer a holistic picture with reference to supervision in any Extension Organisation. Answer any TWO.

1. Discuss the role of supervision in Extension administration with special reference to Indian Scenario.
2. "Extension supervisors do recognise the need of effective delegation as a tool of time management, development and motivation of employees, enhancement of quality and speed of decisions etc.,"— Discuss.
3. "Managerial functions include decision making as one of the vital tasks besides planning and implementation of any development activity". Subordinate.

V. Based on the results given below, offer your interpretation, inferences and implications for Extension supervision:

(Enclosed)

FINAL PRACTICAL

Duration : 3 Hours

Marks : 20

I. Indicate the public, quasi and private sector organisations you visited in connection with this course offer your observations, inferences, major conclusions and implications to research and extension through SWOT analysis. 10

II. Assignments, project works, records etc. 5

III. Viva-Voce 5

Index